Classic
Cricket
Clangers

Other titles in this series

Classic Rugby Clangers

Classic Golf Clangers

Classic Football Clangers

Classic Cricket Clangers

DAVID MORTIMER

ROBSON BOOKS

First published in Great Britain in 2003 by Robson Books,
The Chrysalis Building, Bramley Road, London W10 6SP

Reprinted 2003, 2004

An imprint of **Chrysalis** Books Group plc

Copyright © 2003, 2004 David Mortimer

The right of David Mortimer to be identified as the author of
this work has been asserted by him in accordance with the
Copyright, Designs and Patents Act 1988.

British Library Cataloguing in Publication Data
A catalogue record for this title is available from the
British Library.

ISBN 1 86105 613 3

Typeset by FiSH Books, London
Printed by Creative Print & Design (Wales), Ebbw Vale

Contents

This book is dedicated to all those women who have ever sat freezing on the boundary watching their menfolk being clobbered all over the field, or listening to detailed explanations of why it wasn't really out.

Foreword

'They should burn the scorebooks after every game. Records should not be kept.' So said Arthur Mailey, the great Australian spin bowler, cartoonist, painter, writer and humorist. To him, it was not the sporting facts that mattered, however impressive or derisory, but the human qualities of the players who take part, and the intensely appealing situations the game – any game – can throw up.

When we are spectators at a sporting contest, whether it's a Sunday morning under-11's soccer match on a mudheap of a pitch, or a five-day Test match in the full glare of the international media, we tend to take sides. We are committed, we desire a certain outcome, and the adrenalin flows with the tide of the game. At the time, we briefly note individual moments which shift the balance in favour of one side or another, cheering the good ones, groaning at the bad ones, but having no time to dwell on them. It is only later, in the mellowness of reflection, that we recall those moments of triumph or catastrophe, and begin to humanise them. Of all the sports, perhaps cricket and golf are the best showcases for human interplay, eccentricity, achievement and fallibility. These, after all, are sports in which the outcome is not decided within a hectic hour or two, but is spread over a day, or more usually over three, four and even five days. There is ample time for the tension and mental pressure of the event to build and exert its unpredictable influence on the participants. Sometimes this gives rise to unanticipated brilliance, and the resulting heroics rarely lack their chroniclers.

Just as often, the pressure and tension can produce doubt in unexpected quarters, a crippling moment when the player (or players, since sometimes an entire team suddenly recoils from the steepness of the mountain before it) fails at what might prove to be a career-defining moment. These are the ones we cruelly label chokers. There are others, the jokers, whose response may be bravura, radiating misplaced self-confidence. The end result is generally the same. A moment of embarrassment in which the horrid realisation dawns that you've dropped a clanger – if not for the team then for yourself. Since it is these moments that are less usually chronicled, this little book celebrates – without, I hope, ever directing malice towards its subjects, who have probably suffered enough – some of cricket's red-faced moments, and a few of its more engaging characters, drawn from more than 120 years of the game.

And Wisden Said: 'Let There Be Records'

A bundle of mid-Victorian embarrassments, 1855–82

Reports of matches were sporadic in early and middle Victorian times. Wisden's was not the first cricketers' handbook, but even when his first edition appeared in 1864, its contents could hardly be called topical. It's difficult to pinpoint when cricket writers began to recognise what we now call 'first-class' matches, so for the purposes of this book I've taken the 1870s as the starting point – the decade of the first Test match and of the inaugural county championship – partly because modern Wisdens rarely recognise any record before that date as being worthy of inclusion. Nevertheless, long before the 1870s, cricket exerted that peculiar pull upon the English which was halfway between sport and religion, and there will have been many red-faced participants over whose efforts the local populace, once comfortably inside the nearest inn, must have groaned or shaken their heads in disbelief. With sparse information, often no more than a scorecard, we can only guess at the human drama that might underlie the bare statistics left us by posterity. So, before we get into our stride, here are a few instances from mid-Victorian times that may have caused their perpetrators to lie awake at nights.

In August 1855, the 2nd Royal Surrey Militia was invited to the Earl of Winterton's estate at Shilinglee Park in Sussex for a game against a local side. There would have been heavy betting on the contest, as was the custom (*plus ça change...*), and also some red faces and bristling military moustaches as the Royal Surreys were dismissed without scoring a run. Going in at No 9, Major Ridley upheld the honour of the officer class by contriving to be the not-out batsman, though since Sergeant Ayling, at No 10, was run out for nought, one fancies one can hear the Major's voice echoing down the years: 'Yes. No. Go back. Oh, bad luck, sergeant.'

Nether Stowey fared slightly better against Bishops Lydiard in 1874. Although their batsmen also contrived to miss the ball with conspicuous regularity (they were all clean bowled in just 28 deliveries), they did at least scramble two leg byes. The hero in the inn that night would have been opening batsman C Routley who, in a feat Geoff Boycott would have relished, carried his bat throughout the innings and finished undefeated – on nought.

Charles Absolon was a real old joker. He played in every game of cricket he could lay his studs on, and didn't retire until 1897, when he was 80, by which time he claimed to have done the hat-trick 59 times! So United Willesden were probably none too pleased when he turned up looking for a game with Wood Green one July day in 1872. Whether they lost heart in the face of his reputation or whether he was genuinely too good for them, they collapsed twice – for 24 and 31 – and Absolon took nine wickets in each innings. Bad enough, but he rubbed it in by catching the other two, to claim a hand in all twenty dismissals.

Although it takes us to 1882, spare a thought for Frank Silcock of Rickling Green. He made 14 out of his side's 94 against Orleans, but his main duty was to open the bowling. He cannot have bargained on having to bowl 97 overs (nearly twice as many as anyone else in the side) while G F Vernon (259) and

A H Trevor (338) put on 605 for the second wicket! There was admittedly a bit of a collapse after that, and Orleans only managed 920 all out – not enough to risk asking Rickling to bat again – so the match fizzled out as a tame draw. But poor old Silcock conceded 291 runs in his spell!

But the accolade for supreme Victorian overconfidence surely has to go to Murphy. That's all we know about him, just Murphy, but it wouldn't surprise me if he turned out to be the same Murphy who propagated the famous Law in later life. Opening the batting in April 1867, for the One Leg eleven against the One Arm eleven, he made a pair, nought in each innings, but – and this is his triumph, it seems to me – his first-innings duck was the result of being run out. There's optimism for you. As he might have said himself, at least he wasn't lbw.

'The Wickets Were of Bad Form'

Oxford University v MCC, Oxford, May 1877

Clearly not only the wickets were of bad form as the young gentlemen of Oxford University toodled up to put their names to the lowest score in the history of first class cricket. It is a record that has stood virtually unchallenged for 125 years, although Northamptonshire managed to equal it in 1907 and, in 1983, Surrey came within two runs of it (see page 127).

Of course, one should make due allowance for the state of the wicket since, Wisden stated, 'the match was played in the memorable wet season, and the wickets were of bad form; one end playing very badly.' Graphically put, but despite it one feels the Oxford men's approach was not all it might have been, since their captain, A J Webbe, who would play the next year for England in the Melbourne Test match, was two hours late turning up. Or, as Wisden politely put it (for it was deucedly bad form to criticise a gentleman amateur), 'The Oxford men played without their captain's aid and could not get into their form on such wickets.'

Nor indeed they could. Finding themselves three down for one run, a tenacious stand carried them to eight, at which point another three wickets crashed. This 'jewel of a small innings', as the kindly Wisden called it, finally staggered to 12, of which E W Wallington made a heroic 7 not out. It had required 174 deliveries in two hours to put an end to the agony – or, to put it another way, not only was it bad form, but dashed tedious as well. Maybe the captain did well to oversleep.

For the record, MCC made 124 before skittling the University again for 35, to which the now wide-awake A J Webbe contributed what was, no doubt, a cultured six runs. Fred Morley, also to play for England in years to come, was probably the happiest man on the field that day – his match aggregate was thirteen wickets for fourteen runs! Strangest of all, Oxford went on to win the Varsity match that year.

Tom Emmett Forgets Who Pays His Wages

Yorkshire v Gloucestershire, Sheffield, July 1879

Tom Emmett was one of Yorkshire's finest, but he also had 'the exuberance of the eternal schoolboy'. His playing career spanned that of W G Grace's, and these two figures dominated the cricket field whenever they met just as, according to A A Thomson, 'Gladstone and Disraeli dominated the House of Commons'. As the 1870s began, they had heard of WG up in Yorkshire, of course, but had yet to meet him on home territory. 'He may be all right playing against these second-class counties,' said Tom, 'but wait till he comes to Bramall Lane; we'll show him. Up here, I reckon we'd shoot him before he'd get those sort of scores!'

In July 1872, Gloucestershire finally arrived in Yorkshire. Before they could shoot him, WG made 150 in an opening stand of 238 with T G Matthews. 'He ought to have a littler bat,' growled Tom. The story goes that a man who couldn't get to Sheffield that day, asked his nephew to telegraph him the score at regular intervals. He duly wired, 'Score two hundred for none. Hope to get a wicket any day now.' To rub it in, WG then took eight for 33 and seven for 46.

In 1879, Tom was skipper, and Gloucestershire were back at Bramall Lane needing only 71 for victory. Tom offered team-mate Billy Bates odds of fifty to one that Gloucester, with all three Grace brothers playing, would get them. 'Done,' said Billy, handing over a shilling, and promptly bowled WG for a duck. Thanks to inspired bowling by Peate (six for 40), Gloucester found themselves needing eight to win with just one wicket left. 'I knew what t'last man'd do,' said Tom, 'and I knew Peate'd chuck him one up. So I sneaked right up and took a catch right off his bat-end. And then, for t'first time, I thought of my bet! I reckoned I was lucky to lose only fifty bob. If t'committee knew I'd bet against Yorkshire, it wouldn't half have been awkward!'

Oops, Missed It! Fred Bags a Test Match Pair

England v Australia, the Oval, September 1880

It seems melodramatic to go home and die if you're out for a duck in each innings. It rather draws attention to the mishap. But if the occasion is the first Test match ever played in England, and if you bear one of the most celebrated names in Victorian England, maybe it becomes understandable. Not, mind you, that Fred Grace *meant* to go home and die. It just happened that way.

The fourth Test of all time, and the first on English soil, was very much a last minute affair. A strong group of Australian cricketers was in England, but only a few weeks of the season were left when it was decided to organise a match between the two countries. Naturally enough, W G Grace ('the Champion') would open the batting for England, and two of his brothers were also invited to appear. EM ('the Coroner') put on 91 with WG for the first wicket, WG going on to 152, the first English century-maker in Test history. Fred, who didn't have a nickname, came in to bat with the score at 410 for seven and was promptly snapped up in the slips, whereupon the umpires called time for the day. Bother!

Next day, Fred had a spectacular moment of glory when the giant Aussie hitter, Bonnor, smote the ball prodigiously towards

8

him on the boundary. All accounts agree that when the ball finally returned towards earth his catch was stupendous, and the cheering could be heard on Vauxhall station. When England batted again, needing to knock off only 57 for victory, Fred was asked to open the batting. He appreciated the kind gesture, despite the cold he was developing. He was bowled second ball. Damnation! Undaunted, he set off for another game of cricket, played in the pouring rain, became very ill, and died exactly a fortnight after making Test cricket's first pair.

Who Asked This Feller Briggs Along?

South Africa v England, 2nd Test, Cape Town, March 1889

Johnny Briggs was short and round and one of cricket's tragic figures. Devoted father of twin boys, H S Altham described him as 'one of the most cheerful and loveable personalities in cricket history'. But, in 1899, he would collapse with epilepsy and spend eight months in an asylum. He seemed to recover, but another massive breakdown sent him back to hospital within the year, and he died there in 1902. But that lay in the future. When he joined the English players setting out for South Africa in 1889 as cricketing missionaries, he did so as a good batsman, a fine cover fielder and an outstanding slow left-arm bowler, the master of flight and spin.

The standard of cricket in South Africa was not yet high – perhaps that of a minor county back home. England had been invited so the South Africans could learn, and Johnny in particular taught them more than a few tricks. In the course of the tour he took nearly 300 wickets at five runs apiece. The Englishmen were led by C Aubrey Smith, nicknamed 'Round-the-Corner' Smith because of his peculiar bowling style, who would later become famous as a Hollywood actor. Two Tests had been arranged, and although England won the first comfortably enough, the South Africans were not disgraced. Briggs took six top order wickets, and 'Round-the-Corner' snaffled seven, largely tail-enders, but good enough for him to bore rigid future visitors to Hollywood. The second Test was a somewhat different matter.

Smith contracted fever and passed the captaincy for this Test to wicket-keeper M P Bowden who, aged 23, thus became England's youngest-ever captain. He contrived also to become the shortest-lived England captain. Three years later he died in a large mud hut masquerading as Umtali hospital and, his corpse having been saved from marauding lions, he was buried in a coffin made of whisky cases. History does not record whether he had first disposed of the contents of his coffin material, nor whether (if so) this had anything to do with his death.

By comparison, the second Test was less exotic, although it produced plenty of records. In England's innings, opener Bobby Abel's 120 was the first century to be scored in first class cricket in South Africa. When South Africa replied to England's 292, their opening batsman, A B Tancred, became the first man to carry his bat undefeated through a Test innings. There was only one fly in this otherwise mellifluous ointment. The glow of achievement he may have felt was more than a little dampened by the knowledge that he had only managed 26 not out, and even that was more than the rest of the team put together. South Africa had been shot out for just 47. Johnny Briggs, coming on first change when two wickets were already down, had taken seven for 17, and he had by no means finished his day's work.

The second innings was surely the time for grit and resolution, but when the openers reached the wicket for the second time that day it was to see Johnny beaming at them as he prepared to open the bowling! At this point the South Africans must have asked themselves if they had really wanted to learn that fast, and who asked this Briggs chappie to come anyway? One opener decided he'd rather be in the pavilion and ran himself out at once. Briggs then bowled the hero of the morning, Tancred, for three runs, and he was away. In a mere 14 overs he took eight for 11, all clean bowled, and this time South Africa managed only 43. Thanks to a certain Mr Fothergill chipping in with the remaining wicket (bowled again) this became the first Test innings to be completed without a catch being recorded. In the match, Johnny had taken 15 wickets – the most ever taken in a single day's Test cricket. Fourteen were clean bowled, while the other was lbw – and he probably grumbled about the decision all the way back to the pavilion.

South Africa learned the Briggs lesson fast. Seventeen years later they beat England 4–1, and three years after that by 3–2. They played four spinners, who took the skill to new heights.

Insider Information Can Be Dangerous

Somerset v Surrey, Taunton, 1891

Somerset badly needed a win in 1891, their first year in the county championship. 'First class in classification, at least for the remainder of the season,' The *Sportsman* commented tartly, anticipating a quick return to minor county status. The Victorians evidently had less affection for the underdog than we do today. Surrey came to Taunton that year as reigning champions – indeed they had worn the crown for four years and were to retain it for two more, so it seemed improbable that Somerset's badly needed win would come in this match. They had reckoned without S M J Woods, or Sam as he was universally known.

Sam was born in Australia, one of a family of thirteen. 'At least, I *think* we were thirteen,' he would say. He came to school in England when he was fourteen, went on to Cambridge and played for Australia in three Tests in 1888 while still an undergraduate. He also played rugby for England, soccer for the Corinthians and, if he needed other amusements, would indulge with distinction in hockey, boxing, billiards, hammer-throwing, shot-putting – and skittles. It was skittle-playing in a Somerset pub that reflected his true nature, and indeed he liked Somerset pubs so well that for many years he lived in one. Sam knew every inch of Somerset ground and seemed to know every one of its inhabitants. In winter he would keep fit by following the hounds on foot and, to make sure he and his companions would never go thirsty, secreted bottles of beer under hedges, in rabbit holes, in hollow tree trunks, and remembered each hiding place with the infallibility of a dog retrieving a buried bone. 'Everyone loved Sam,' wrote R C Robertson-Glasgow, a later Somerset player who knew him well. 'The whole world's manliness and generosity seemed to have gathered into his heart.'

There was probably only one thing Sam could not abide, and that was a drawn cricket match. On one occasion, when captaining the Gentlemen against the Players in the annual showcase match at Lords, he had set his opponents 500 to win. At the end of what should have been the last over, the scores were level, and the Players had two wickets in hand. The umpires advanced on the wickets to remove the bails and call time, but Sam snatched the ball and insisted on another over. The Players duly got the run they needed and won the match. 'Draws are only good for swimming in,' was all he had to say on the matter.

But to return to 1891. Surrey, the champions, were playing the new boys on the county circuit, and Somerset were tantalisingly close to the victory they wanted so badly. Sam had the ball in his hand to begin the last over and Surrey, with only a draw to play for, had their last pair, H Wood and J W Sharpe, hanging on. Sharpe was a pretty fair opening bowler, good enough to partner the great Lockwood in the attack, and to take 275 wickets at an average of 15.2 in his five years with Surrey. He was not so sharp with the bat, though, and mustered a total of only 503 runs in his 79 innings for the club. Wood was in his eighth season with Surrey, and although he was to play on for another nine years, he was generally only dusted down and brought out when Surrey needed to make up the numbers against the lesser fry.

Sam put down two good, quick deliveries. Sharpe got behind them both with no apparent difficulty and kept them out. At the bowler's end Wood, the other batsman, chuckled and said to Sam as he unwittingly prepared to hand the match to Somerset, all neatly gift-wrapped: 'Keeps his end up pretty well for a man with only one eye, don't he?' 'Yes, indeed,' answered Sam. 'Do you know I've clean forgotten which eye it is?' And Wood, who clearly loved to be of service, replied, 'It's the left one, poor chap.'

After the passage of more than a century, we can only imagine the thoughtful look that must have flitted over Sam's face at this point. 'Then, you know,' Sam related later, 'I bowled the first round-arm ball of my life and hit his off stump!'

Australia Collapse on the Brink of Victory

Australia v England, 1st Test, Sydney, December 1894

Headingley and Edgbaston in 1981 and the Oval in 1997. Occasions when England not only put it across the old enemy but had the pleasure of wrenching apparently certain victory from their grasp. Australians rarely choke on anything, least of all in sport, so followers of England tend to think of Headingley, Edgbaston and the Oval as a unique trio of victories, but something very similar happened way back in 1894, and on Australian soil at that.

The England touring party of 1894–5 was skippered by A E Stoddart. It included the imperious Lancastrian Archie MacLaren, soon to make 424 against Somerset, a score that would not be bettered in England for 99 years; J T Brown, 'the pride of Yorkshire', who in 1898 would share in a record first-wicket stand of 554 against Derbyshire; and Surrey's mighty fast bowler Tom Richardson, who had taken ten wickets in an innings the previous June. England had lost a three-Test series in Australia in 1891–2, but beaten the Australians 1–0 on their visit to England in 1893. Stoddart's team was therefore awaited in 1894 with immense excitement and, for only the second time, the series was expanded to five Tests. There were capacity crowds wherever England played, and the Test scores were wired across Australia to be displayed on boards in city squares.

At its close, the first Test was described as 'probably the most sensational match ever played either in Australia or England'. It began disastrously for Australia who in no time were 21 for three, with Tom Richardson clean bowling Trott, Lyons and Darling. That was the end of English celebrations, as first Iredale (81) and Giffen (161) put on 171 for the fourth wicket, and Giffen and Syd Gregory (201) put on 139 for the fifth wicket. Gregory's was only the second double-century scored in eighteen years of Test match cricket, and it took him only four hours. Australia finished on 586, Richardson having taken five for 181 in 55.3 overs, an astonishing effort in the summer heat and humidity of Sydney.

In a description to become familiar during the next century, England's first innings was workmanlike. Hardly anybody failed, but only Lancastrian Albert Ward (75) stuck for any length of time, and England finished with 325. The pitch was a little easier as they followed on in the second innings. Once again Ward led the way, this time scoring 117, and he and Johnnie Brown (53) enjoyed a Roses partnership of 102 as England fought their way to 437 by the afternoon of the fourth day. Was it enough to save the day in this high-scoring match? Australia needed just 177.

At close of play they were 113 for two, with Giffen and Darling well set. That evening the English players 'relaxed', believing the game irretrievably lost. Yorkshire's Bobby Peel was especially celebrated for his ability to relax, and managed it so comprehensively that captain Stoddart sobered him up under a cold shower. During the night the rain fell, the wicket turned helpful, and Australian nerves tightened in face of a target of 64 runs, despite eight wickets in hand. In what was described as 'nerve-shattering cricket' Peel took six for 67, and Australia were all out for 166, eleven short of their objective.

This was the prelude to one of the most enthralling of all Ashes series. England went two up in Melbourne before (with a somewhat modern overtone) their batting collapsed in the third and fourth tests with successive totals of 124, 143, 65 and 72. The series stood all square therefore as they began the final Test, billed as 'the match of the century'. Australia scored 414, England replied with 385, and then bowled Australia out for 267, Tom Richardson taking six for 104. Needing 297, they lost two quick wickets before Johnnie Brown came in, hit his first two balls for four, reached his fifty in 28 minutes (still a Test match record) and his century in 95 minutes. When he was out for 140 and Ward for 93 after a stand of 210, England were poised for a thrilling victory by six wickets to retain the Ashes.

The Guv'nor Fails to Enjoy WG's Birthday Bash

Gentlemen v Players, Lord's, July 1898

In 1898 the Champion, W G Grace, celebrated his fiftieth birthday. He had enjoyed his *annus mirabilis* only three years earlier when he had become the first batsman to score a thousand runs in May, and the first to reach a hundred centuries (with a score of 288, which he followed a few days later with one of 257). The question being hotly debated as the 1898 season began was how best to mark his jubilee. In those days, when Test matches were relatively new-fangled affairs, the great cricketing events were the twice-yearly contests between the amateurs and the professionals. Someone had the bright idea, roundly applauded, of delaying the Gentlemen versus the Players game at Lord's so that it would coincide with WG's birthday, 18 July.

As usual, each side picked its strongest eleven. WG, also known as 'the Doctor', would captain the Gentlemen, naturally, and although they were hardly on speaking terms at the time, the feared Kortright would open the bowling. Despite the absence of any means of measurement, legend has it, even today, that Kortright was the fastest bowler of all time. There was no subtlety about him. His run up was twenty strides. He had no interest in the novel ideas of swing or seam bowling. He simply roared up to the wicket and, without a discernible check in his delivery stride, hurled the ball down as fast as he could. There is a story that one young batsman stood awaiting Kortright's first delivery with his left heel on the ground and the toe in the air, in the manner of WG. Kortright stopped in his run-up and addressed him: 'Nobody except the Doctor puts his toe in the air when I'm bowling to him!' The young man laughed politely but failed to alter his stance, whereupon Kortright delivered a yorker on the point of his big toe. He was not seen at the wicket again for several weeks.

Opening the batting for the Players was little Bobby Abel, affectionately known to his home crowd at the Oval as 'the Guv'nor'. He had, a contemporary wrote, 'a quaint birdlike appearance – the roundness of a robin and the self-assertion of a cock-sparrow – with a sidelong waddle to and from the wicket.' But he could score runs, my goodness he could. The very next year he would make 357 not out, then the second biggest innings ever played. He already had eleven England caps and, as usual, he was near the top of the national batting averages. The only fly in the Guv'nor's ointment was that he didn't like fast bowling – not really fast bowling. But like it or not, he was about to encounter it!

Twenty thousand spectators crammed into Lord's to watch Abel and Shrewsbury open the Players' first innings. One of them reckoned Kortright 'let himself go like a steam engine', and the Guv'nor did not enjoy the sensation, repeatedly backing away towards square leg. After three-quarters of an hour the score was 25, of which Abel had managed just seven, and it was with difficulty that both openers had kept their heads intact. Ribs were a different matter, and Abel was still recovering from a blow in the chest when he found himself facing Kortright again, prodded hopefully forward and heard his leg stump leave the ground. Thanks to William Gunn's 139, the Players reached

335 and bowled the Gentlemen out for 303 (WG made 43) before Abel's torment began again.

The Players had fifty minutes of the second day's play to negotiate, and the light was not good. Spectators debated whether Kortright would be charged with murder or manslaughter as he charged in from the pavilion end, then without a sightscreen of any kind. This time Abel lasted ten minutes for five runs before he departed in obvious relief. In the pavilion, Lyttleton thought it was painful to see a batsman so obviously running away from the bowler. But with a logic which would resonate with the England players of 2001 when faced with a tour to India during the bombing of nearby Afghanistan, Abel merely commented, 'Well, I'm the father of six children, and there are plenty of bowlers to score runs off besides Mr Kortright.'

You Can't Bowl That, It Hasn't Been Invented!

Middlesex v Leicestershire, Lord's, July 1900

Bernard Bosanquet, inventor of the googly (still called 'the bosie' by Australians), was the perfect example of the gentleman-cricketer of the Edwardian 'Golden Age'. As his son, the TV presenter Reginald, said, he 'drifted from one country-house party to the next, tipping the butler on Monday morning, before travelling to his next social-cum-sporting invitation'. He whiled away the longueurs by perfecting the art of spinning a ball with an action that seemed to indicate orthodox turn in one direction whilst actually making it go in the opposite.

Bosanquet spent a couple of years practising this sinful delivery which, as a later commentator observed, 'corrupted the innocence of the days when predictability was expected', before deciding he was ready to try it out on some unfortunate victim.

Unsuspecting Leicestershire were selected. They had been elevated to first-class status only six years earlier but, though finding victories hard to come by, had had the temerity to beat Middlesex in their home encounter earlier in the year, with their talented left-hander, Sam Coe (80), top-scoring.

When Leicester came back to Lord's, Bosanquet had already made 136 in under two hours in Middlesex's first innings (and was to make 137 in the second), and was therefore in a mood to try anything when he was tossed the ball to have a bowl at Coe. The excellent Sam was on 98, and the certainty of three figures must have flashed before him as he observed this fresh-faced youth, newly down from university, amble up. It's unlikely that he spotted the googly. It was, after all, receiving its unadvertised public baptism. If he had, he would no doubt have considered it a scurrilous, underhand trick. As it was, it was the bounce – or rather, the bounces – that beat him. However fiendishly it may or may not have turned, it bounced four times before bowling him. Poor Sam traipsed off with the hoots of Middlesex merriment ringing in his ears.

Clem Gets Nervous in the Nineties

Australia v England, 2nd & 3rd Tests, Melbourne/Adelaide, January 1902

Clem Hill was not a nervous sort of chap – indeed he was quite a pugnacious little fellow. In 1912, he would be a central figure in a raging dispute with the new Australian Board of Control that resulted in 'The Big Six' players missing that year's tour of England. He made some of his points so vigorously that he blacked the eye of a Board member in the process. Perhaps this truculent spirit helped make him one of Australia's best left-handed batsmen ever. He'd already scored two of his seven test centuries before the 1901–2 series against England began in Australia. The public confidently anticipated at least one more ton from Clem.

England went into the second Test in Melbourne 1–0 up. There, on a sticky wicket, Australia reversed their batting order for the second innings and, going in at No 7, Clem was out for 99, the first time anyone had suffered that fate in a Test. When the teams locked horns again for the Test in Adelaide, he was back in his usual No 3 position and, batting fluently, was easily Australia's top scorer. This time he would surely get the ton he'd been denied in Melbourne. But no! On 98, opening bowler Len Braund came back on and had him caught.

When they batted again, Australia wanted 315, at that time easily the biggest fourth innings total required for victory. Once again, Hill top-scored in the run chase; once again he powered his way into the nineties; and once again, unbelievably, he fell – this time for 97, bowled by Gilbert Jessop. This extraordinary sequence of scores – 99, 98, 97 – has never been so precisely repeated. Australia took the series 4–1, but the ebullient Hill must have gone to his grave wondering how he could have dropped three clangers in a row.

'We've Got You This Time, Joe'

England v Australia, 4th Test, Old Trafford, 1902

The Cornstalks, as the 1902 Australians were nicknamed, ran into one of England's wettest summers. In the first Test, England had skittled them for 36, Australia's lowest Test score to this day, and had them 46 for two in the second innings, still 293 short of avoiding an innings defeat, when rain killed the game. In the second Test at Lord's, the weather allowed only 105 minutes' play. The third Test was played in Sheffield, the 'smokestack city', where the workers stoked up the furnaces to reduce the visibility when Yorkshire's opponents were batting. England lost by 143 runs, and went to Manchester one down with two to play.

For the selectors the bowling, not the batting, was problematical, especially as Yorkshire refused to release more than three players for the national side. The name of Fred Tate, then heading the national averages, came up in committee, but Tate was a medium-pacer at his best on fast dry pitches. He was, moreover, a specialist slip fielder (the team already had three), and even his best friends could only look away when his batting was mentioned. His name was therefore not in the eleven chosen. But when rain set in, two days before the match,

Tate was illogically added to the team list. On the day itself, he duly won his first – and only – Test cap.

The match began on a damp pitch with the sun starting to appear. Losing the toss, Archie McLaren, the England captain, told his players, 'It's all right, boys, they're batting; the sun's coming out; we've only got to keep 'em quiet till lunch, and then the pitch'll be sticky and we'll bowl 'em out as quick as they come in. So keep Victor quiet at all costs!'

McLaren's analysis was right, but the execution of this master plan went a little astray. At lunch, Australia were 173 for one, the glorious Victor Trumper 103 not out. A century before lunch in a Test match had been thought an impossible feat until now. In later years, McLaren would entertain lunch guests with demonstrations of the cunning fields he had set for Trumper, using glasses, ashtrays and pepper pots as surrogate fielders. 'And Victor just hit it over the top of 'em!' he would chuckle. After the magnificence of the morning session, Australia struggled grimly thereafter and were eventually all out for 299. Fred Tate took none for 44 in eleven overs.

In reply, England were 44 for four on the treacherous wicket but, thanks to a superb 128 by F S Jackson as the conditions eased, finished only 37 behind on 262. It was essential to capture quick Aussie wickets in the second innings, and Lockwood (five for 28) whipped out the first three for just ten runs, to bring in left-handed skipper, Joe Darling. With the score 16, and one ball of the over left, McLaren moved Fred Tate from slip to square leg for just one delivery. Darling mis-hit massively, the ball swirled hideously in the air, and Tate dropped it. Darling's partnership with Syd Gregory put on 54, by far the biggest stand of the innings, and Australia were all out for 86 (Tate taking two for seven and a slick slip catch). England needed 124 to win.

At 92 for three they seemed home and dry. 'We've got you this time, Joe,' said McLaren to Darling in the tea interval. 'The rest of you will shiver with fright,' was the reply. Sure enough, the middle order collapsed and, at 116 for nine, Tate came out to join Wilfred Rhodes. Immediately, a 45-minute rain break stretched the nerves tighter. Then Tate's ordeal began. His first ball was snicked for four. Four more needed. He blocked the second and third, but the fourth ball, keeping low, took his leg stump. Australia had won by three runs and kept the Ashes.

It was Trumper's brilliance on the first morning that won the match for Australia, but the public wanted a scapegoat and Tate, the slip fielder who'd dropped a skier at square leg, and the No 11 who'd failed to score eight on a wearing wicket, would do nicely. But Fred's son, Maurice, more than avenged his father. Between the wars, he took 155 wickets in 39 Tests, and a good few of them were Australian.

This New Kind of Bowling is a Very Great Invention

South Africa steals the googly, 1906–10

When Bosanquet invented the googly (see page 22), he can't have imagined that it would so soon be turned against his own countrymen. His own Test career was a short one of just seven matches, all against Australia, and he enjoyed only fitful success but, at around the time he was launching his new delivery with Middlesex, he became friendly with Reginald Schwarz. The two played together for the county, and also toured the USA in 1901. In the following year, Schwarz took up an appointment in South Africa, and there he shared the secret of the googly with Ernie Vogler, Aubrey Faulkner and Gordon White. These four musketeers were to give English batsmen a torrid time in the thirteen Tests between January 1906 and March 1910, South Africa winning seven of them to England's four.

England were served notice of the new threat on their tour of South Africa in 1906. To be fair, it was not a strong side that made the tour, but on the matting wickets of Johannesburg and Cape Town they were resoundingly beaten 4–1, and South Africa's googly quartet captured exactly half the wickets to fall. Back home in London, it was easy to minimise the threat they posed. It had not been a full England side, and on matting wickets the steepness with which the ball bounces meant the batsman had to play the ball chest high, a difficult proposition against any kind of spin. It would all be different when South Africa came to England in 1907 and played on proper wickets.

1907 was a very wet summer, and the wickets were consistently soft which, in the event, played into the hands of the googly quartet. Of the fifty English wickets to fall in the three-match Test series, they bagged forty. In the second and third Tests, South Africa opened with spin at each end, and in the third both their first-change bowlers were googly merchants. Not even in the 1970s heyday of India's great spin bowlers did a side so comprehensively dismiss the apparent disadvantage of the new ball to the spinner.

The legendary R E Foster, scorer of 287 not out against Australia in his first Test, was captain of England in the 1907 series and had a wretched time against South Africa with the bat. Although he managed 51 in the third Test it was, apparently, an embarrassing knock, full of snicks between pad and wicket, or through the slips. He reckoned Vogler the finest bowler of the quartet. His stock ball was the leg break, but roughly every other over he would bowl a googly. 'It is almost impossible to see this ball coming. After very careful watching the only difference one can detect, and this is possibly fancy, is that the hand seems to be turned farther over in the action of delivery.'

All the England batsmen agreed that the great feature of all four googly bowlers was the extraordinary way in which the ball gathered speed after pitching. 'It was,' said one player, 'like playing Briggs through the air and Richardson off the pitch,' or, in contemporary terms, Warne through the air and McGrath off the pitch. In South Africa they had assumed it was the effect of matting laid over hard, compacted ground or gravel, but when the same phenomenon was encountered on soft English wickets, other reasons had to be found. 'A possible cause may be that the South Africans seem to deliver the ball with a flick, relying entirely on finger and wrist for spin,' thought Foster. Whatever the reason, the spin imparted made the ball fizz off the turf disconcertingly. Despite being dismissed for 76 and 162 at Lord's, England were saved from humiliation by South African batting that was even weaker than their own, and took the series 1–0.

When they sent another side to South Africa in 1909–10, the history of their earlier tour repeated itself when they were faced once more by the googly quartet, though they did manage to reduce the margin of defeat to 3–2 on this occasion. That they did so was largely thanks to one man – the young Jack Hobbs – who seemed able to understand the black art of the googly in a way that eluded the rest of the side. Their successful struggles with England represented the high-water mark of the great quartet and, oddly, South Africa never again produced a great googly bowler.

Days of Glory That Ended With a Pistol Shot

Middlesex v Somerset, Lord's, Whit Monday 1907

Albert Trott's is a sad and bitter story, unfitting for a genial, mischievous Australian who liked his pint. He had, mind you, days of astonishing achievement to look back on, quite apart from his unique six over the pavilion at Lord's. In the thrilling Ashes series of 1894–5 (see page 16), he was brought into the Australian side for the third Test and turned the series around with eight for 43, and innings of 38 and 72, both not out, which he followed in the fourth Test with an undefeated 85 to help square the series and set up the astonishing finale in Melbourne.

Unaccountably ignored by the Aussie selectors for the 1896 tour to England, this 'hard-hitting batsman, overwhelming fast-medium bowler and safe catcher with huge hands' packed his bags and arrived at Lord's to make his living from cricket with Middlesex. For three or four years he made a very good fist of it, taking 239 wickets and scoring 1,175 runs in 1899, and 211 wickets and 1,337 runs in 1900, but from 1902 on his performances began to decline as his physique gradually deteriorated.

One autumnal flash of glory lay ahead. He was popular at Lord's, and in 1907 he was given a benefit match against Somerset. In those far-off, pre-social security days, this was a

32

vital chance to earn a pension for later years, so you prayed for good weather, big crowds and a match that went to the last ball. At this crucial moment of his life, Albert dropped a cartload of clangers, all of them in a single day's play. He started by taking four wickets in four balls, and rounded matters off in double-quick time by doing a hat-trick to dismiss what was left of Somerset before the first day's play had run its course. The crowds cheered, but the kitty was small.

Trott became an umpire, but ill health forced his retirement, and five days before the start of World War I he shot himself. His only possessions were a wardrobe and four one pound notes.

'I Think I Know How to Beat Armstrong's Lot'

A C McLaren's XI v Australians, Eastbourne, August 1921

Those who chatted to Warwick Armstrong, the 'Big Ship', towards the end of his life thought they detected a moist eye when he reminisced about England, but as an Australian player before World War I, and as captain in 1920–1, his reputation was one of hard-eyed ruthlessness. Having annihilated England down under by an unprecedented margin of 5–0, he brought his Australians to England in the summer of 1921 determined to win every match. And indeed McDonald and Gregory, his magnificent pair of fast bowlers, won the first three Tests for him by huge margins. England, who tried a record thirty players in the series, finally found a combination that could at least stem the flow of disasters and, helped by dead wickets, held out for draws in the last two Tests. The counties were all swept away by the Big Ship's bow wave.

'I think I know how to beat Armstrong's lot,' Archie McLaren wrote to Neville Cardus. 'Come and write about it for the *Guardian*.' Cardus's editor was not so sure. McLaren's career was over, the Australians had conquered contemptuously wherever they had set foot, and were not likely to be challenged by Archie's amateurs. There were more important things to write about as the county championship reached its denouement. In the end Cardus got grudging approval, and he was the only newspaper reporter present.

There was no question of the Australians intending anything other than outright victory, and they had their full Test side out. They also had McLaren's amateurs out in double-quick time (an hour and a quarter, to be precise) for 43, McDonald taking five for 21 on a wicket described as perfect. By the end of the day they themselves were out for 174, and the match, as Cardus realised, was as good as over. 'I knew I was to become a weekend's laughing stock in the eyes of my colleagues and the press at large,' and indeed in the *Manchester Guardian* it was his deputy's report of the Essex v Lancashire match that had pride of place.

But for the sake of nostalgia he went to the ground on Monday morning to see McLaren, his childhood hero, open the batting for the last time in his career. Then he would take the morning train back to London and seek to salvage his reputation. McLaren was bowled for five, and Cardus began, very slowly, to move towards the exit. But something held him back. Aubrey Faulkner, the great South African all-rounder (see page 29) was at the wicket, and he seemed to be taking command. When he was joined by Hubert Ashton, with the score at 60, a change came over the innings. Cardus began to retrace his steps. He did not go to London that day – nor indeed the next.

In the last big innings of his life, Faulkner (153) put on 154 with Ashton (75), and 'Archie's innocents' as they had been christened after the first innings debacle, were all out for 326, setting the Australians 196 to win.

On the final day the bowlers, inspired by their batsmen's fighting performance, gained the confidence they had lacked before, and none more so than C H Gibson of Cambridge University (six for 64), as he dismissed 'Horseshoe' Collins and Warren Bardsley, the run-maker of the first innings. The turning point, in Wisden's opinion, came when Charlie McCartney was bowled by a beauty with the score on 73. Now the Australians, the stranglers of the first day, were struggling. Perhaps they had relaxed mentally after the ease with which they had brushed their opponents aside in their first innings but, Cardus wrote, they 'would have given hairs from their heads to save themselves'. The fact remained that, after nine months of continuous domination, they were unable to scale this last height. They still required 42 runs when Aubrey Faulkner, the last of South Africa's great googly quartet, trapped the 'Big Ship' plumb in front, and when Gibson bowled Arthur Mailey, the Australians had lost by 28. 'The sensation of the season,' said Wisden. Cardus's faith had been rewarded, and he had the only scoop of his journalistic life. 'I saw McLaren coming from the field, conqueror in the last great match of his career in England, his sweater hung about his shoulders and his grey head bared to the crowd as he raised his cap to acknowledge their acclamations.'

'How About a Spot of Golf When We've Got You Out Again?'

Warwickshire v Hampshire, Edgbaston, June 1922

'I say, old chap,' said the Hon. F S G Calthorpe, captain of Warwickshire, to the Hon. Lionel Tennyson, his opposite number on the Hampshire side, on the evening of the first day, 'how about a spot of golf tomorrow morning when we've got you out again?' These may not have been his exact words, but despite the fact that his side had just been dismissed in less than nine overs for 15 (yes, fifteen), they were sufficient to rouse the combustible Tennyson to what John Arlott called 'peaks of profanity' – and, what's more, to place an immediate bet (at long odds) on a Hampshire victory.

Even to those familiar with Tennyson's impetuosity, his wager must have seemed somewhat on the rash side. Warwickshire had scored 223 on a wicket which, though it was turning slowly, was comfortable for batting, and must then have pinched themselves at regular intervals as Hampshire went from nought for three to five for five and then ten for eight before a monumental eighth wicket stand of five enabled them to scale the dizzy heights of fifteen. They had already lost a further two wickets, following on, before Calthorpe's provocative proposal. Tennyson's determination was further fuelled as he read some of the offerings in his mail the next morning. Clearly, Hampshire's plight had tickled the nation's funny bone, and Tennyson received a number of suggestions about activities in which his side might enjoy greater success, one of which proposed painting spots on rocking horses.

But despite his determination and self-assurance, Tennyson himself was out for a hard-hitting 45, and Hampshire's sixth wicket went down with 31 still needed to avoid an innings defeat. It was not reasonable to think even of saving the game; to profess winning it would be deemed lunatic – and this was exactly the kind of thing that the great George Brown relished. As John Arlott rarely tired of telling the world, Brown was the most complete all-round cricketer the game has known. He opened the batting for England and, although not Hampshire's regular wicket-keeper, he kept for England against South Africa and Australia. He was a brilliant fielder and, especially in his early days, often opened the bowling for Hampshire at genuine pace. 'He was at his best when the battle was hottest. He thrived on challenge,' said Arlott. On this day, he was batting at No 4, the challenge was on, and it was the Hon. F S G Calthorpe who was going to choke on it.

When Walter Livsey came in to join George Brown, the score was 274 for eight and Hampshire were just 66 ahead. That season, Livsey, a nervous starter, played 36 innings in all and, this one game apart, made just 181 runs. Clearly, little could be expected of him, the new ball was due shortly and, notwithstanding George Brown, a Warwickshire victory was simply a matter of time. Brown, of course, had other ideas. While continuing to attack the bowlers, he also farmed the bowling cleverly, keeping Livsey away from the strike and, unaccountably, Calthorpe failed to take the new ball – a clanger which 'Tiger' Smith, the Warwickshire wicket-keeper, always reckoned cost them the match. Gradually Livsey's confidence grew in a partnership of 177, and by the time Brown was bowled for 172, aiming to drive through mid-on, Livsey was in sight of his own century. He reached it in a last-wicket stand of 70, and was 110 not out when the Hampshire innings finally closed on 521, setting Warwickshire 314 to win.

At 77 for one, with the third day drifting away, it looked for a while as if Tennyson might be denied the fruits of his extravagant wager. Then, suddenly, the breakthrough came, and in the next hour five wickets went down for 12 runs. Warwickshire were looking down both barrels. Calthorpe, whose captaincy had cost his side the match, tried to make amends with a battling 30, but it was too late. Hampshire won by 155 runs – possibly the most improbable victory of all time. 'At the end, Lionel (Tennyson) could no longer restrain his delight,' said H L V Day, Hampshire's No 3. 'I can recollect his glistening figure giving a passable imitation of a Highland Fling under the shower.' Never lacking in hospitality, Tennyson put his winnings to fluid use that night, and the party was as expansive as his personality. All very well for Hampshire – they were not playing again for four days. But poor, punch-drunk Warwickshire were due in the middle again for an away game the very next morning!

'O Rare George Gunn!'

How he missed the boat,
1920

In George Gunn's opinion, cricket was made for man, not the other way around. It was there to be enjoyed by those who played, and they should never be enslaved by it. Either side of World War I, he would often open the batting for Nottinghamshire. How long he stayed at the crease depended on his mood and the strength of the opposition. If it was a lovely morning, the pitch was true, the bowling ordinary and he fancied sitting in a deck chair with his family, he would quite likely be out in short order. On one occasion, at Edgbaston, resplendent in white panama hat, he scored twenty imperious runs in less than fifteen minutes before daintily patting a half-volley back to the bowler. 'What on earth were you doing getting out to that, George?' his captain asked. 'Too hot, sir,' was George's reply. There were, as he often said, plenty of good batsmen in the side who could score the runs the skipper wanted.

Life in the Gunn household had its summertime routines. One of them was that, round about eight o'clock during home matches, Mrs Gunn would take George his breakfast and the papers to enjoy in bed. On the second morning of one particular county game, in which Notts had started their innings the previous evening, Mrs Gunn realised, round about quarter past ten, that she had heard no sound of George getting up. George had dozed off over the paper, and being shaken awake by his wife with urgent injunctions to get to the ground, said, 'Never mind. We've more runs to get yet. Skipper'll let 'em bat till lunch at least.' 'But George,' replied Mrs Gunn, 'you're 63 not out!' George looked in his paper to verify this information and, finding it to be true, agreed to get up.

But this was also the man who would walk down the wicket to the fastest bowlers and glance or drive them, much as Ted Dexter treated Wes Hall and Charlie Griffith at Lords in 1963. This was the man who, at the age of 28, was recuperating from illness in Australia in 1907–8 when a desperate England side summoned this uncapped player to come and help them in an hour of need in the first Test at Sydney. In the first innings he scored 119, out of a total of 273, a knock which took only 150 minutes, contained twenty boundaries and which, according to Wisden, was 'as nearly as possible faultless'. For good measure, he top-scored in the second innings as well, with 74. Having discovered this treasure almost by accident, England kept him for the whole series, and he repaid them with another century in the fifth Test.

He toured Australia a second time in the triumphant 1911–12 series – and didn't play again for England for eighteen years when, at the age of 50, he toured the West Indies (and shared an opening partnership of 173 with Andrew Sandham in the fourth Test)! In the meantime, he continued to please himself about the way he bestowed his rich talents. He seemed to reserve his most arbitrary displays for Yorkshire, in those days far and away the most powerful of the county teams. Perhaps it was his resolve to show the Tykes how dull 'business' cricket could be, or perhaps he relished their frustration. On one such occasion, facing a mountainous Yorkshire first innings, he batted all day for 100 not out, savouring the sarcastic sledging of the Yorkshire fielders about his slowness. Having thoroughly annoyed and frustrated them, he went out in the second innings and in under two hours scored 108 not out. No other Notts batsman reached double figures. That was George Gunn all over!

So why did this unpredictable genius wait eighteen years for an England recall? According to legend, George was handed an envelope during a county game at Trent Bridge towards the end of August 1920. He stuffed it in his jacket pocket and only found it again when he turned up for pre-season practice the following year. It had contained an invitation to tour Australia that winter as a member of Johnny Douglas's England team. No wonder John Arlott called him 'O Rare George Gunn'.

'Who'd A' Thowt It?'

Yorkshire v Lancashire, Headingley, June 1924; Bradford, May 1926

Even today, Yorkshire and Lancashire meet in Roses matches like two front rows thudding into each other at Twickenham, but between the two world wars the twice-yearly Roses battles were, metaphorically, fights to the death. 'Tha' knows,' Yorkshire's Roy Kilner said, 'the two teams turns up on Bank Holiday, and we all meets in t'dressin' room, and we all says "Good mornin'" to one another. And then we never speaks again for three days!' Not so much as an inch was willingly given or conceded by either side.

The 1924 battle at Headingley began in the way dictated by old-established custom. On a slow, but by no means difficult, wicket Lancashire had scored just 39 runs by the time the lunch interval caused a break in the 'entertainment', and this was thought to be properly decorous by those in attendance. Lancashire plodded on to a total of 113 all out, and on the following day Yorkshire positively skittered to 130 in a mere three and a half hours before Lancashire's second attempt was, as Neville Cardus wrote in the *Manchester Guardian* the following day, 'born into a sea of troubles' on a wicket by now sticky and treacherous. To the unfettered joy of the Yorkshire

43

crowd, it did not detain them long. By the close, Lancashire were all out for 74, leaving Yorkshire the whole of the third day to knock off the 58 needed for victory. Even by the standards of a Roses match, this would provide ample time.

At the time, that fine cricket writer A A Thomson, a Yorkshireman to the depths of his being, was living in Essex and, needing to go to London that afternoon, drove to Bishop's Stortford to catch the train. Wanting to know if Yorkshire had won by nine wickets or ten, he bought an early-evening paper and turned to the Stop Press. 'Ridiculous,' he muttered to himself, and bought a different paper. This confirmed the unbelievable. Yorkshire were all out for 33. His train came in, and went out again as he paced the platform trying to comprehend this reversal of the natural order of things. 'For an instant, I contemplated hurling myself under the next one. Perhaps it was fortunate it was not due for three and a half hours.'

For Cardus, as determinedly Lancastrian as Thomson was Tyke, the sensations were of quite a different sort. 'Not even the annals of Lancashire cricket contain a page more thrilling, more splendid, than the one written today,' he exulted in the paper next morning. His customary impartiality was abandoned as he described with glee the reaction of the Yorkshire crowd to the clatter of wickets. 'It was an affable crowd – how it laughed as a small dog followed at the heels of the cricketers as they walked out. And then came the thunderbolts, out of the blue sky of everybody's complacence.' Sutcliffe fell for three; Holmes, his great partner, for a duck; Maurice Leyland for another. Three wickets for three runs. Abandoning their customary approach to Roses cricket, the Yorkshire batsmen began to hit recklessly – but unavailingly. At 13 for five, a man in the crowd said, with an air of profound certainty, 'It's a funny game is cricket.' At 32 for eight, he stood up and declared: 'That's done it. I'm off. Who'd a' thowt it?' Who indeed? In that day and age, who would ever have expected a

Yorkshire side to surrender in less than 24 overs on a wicket no worse, and possibly a little easier, than that on which they had dismissed the archenemy for 74 the previous day?

The first Roses game of 1926 could scarcely have been more different for Yorkshire as they piled on 326 in seven hours, with Kilner (85) and Edgar Oldroyd (64), grandfather of Radio 4's sports commentator, Eleanor Oldroyd, top-scoring.

In reply, Lancashire struggled painfully towards 153. 'Oh, the royal agony of these Lancashire and Yorkshire matches!' wrote Cardus, still on duty for the *Guardian*. 'Why did Lancashire's later batsmen throw wickets to the wind with the follow-on almost saved?' But this was as nothing to his despair on the third and final day. Rain delayed play until three o'clock, leaving Lancashire just over three hours to save the game – and a Roses game at that. They were all out for 73, wilting unpardonably in the face of Kilner, who took four for 19 with his left-arm leg-spin. In next day's *Guardian*, Cardus penned an excoriating condemnation of Lancashire's spineless performance. 'How is it that any county cricketer, with seasons of experience behind him, is unable to find a little acquaintance with the very rudiments of batting?'

Ironically, Lancashire went on to become county champions that year, but it meant nothing to Yorkshiremen. How could Lancashire be considered champions when they had failed to win the Roses games?

The Man Who Bowled a Nobel Prize Winner

Northamptonshire v Dublin University, July 1926

S C Adams belongs to the exclusive band to have taken a wicket with their first ball in a first-class match. His career was otherwise thoroughly undistinguished, punctuated by the clangings of missed opportunity. Between 1926 and 1932 he appeared as an amateur in a handful of matches for Northamptonshire, achieving a career aggregate of 146 runs and 13 wickets. Out of this paltry total, 87 runs and 6 wickets came in a single game against Dublin University. What lifts him triumphantly onto a pedestal is that (although he would not live to know it, as he died in World War II) he is the only one of the 'First-Ball Wicket' club to claim as his victim a Nobel laureate.

Samuel Beckett (*Waiting for Godot*, *Krapp's Last Tape*, etc.) played cricket at school and at Trinity College in Dublin, and was a good enough all-rounder to play for the University against Northants in 1925 and 1926. The 1925 game was lost (Beckett 18 and 12, and nought for 17 in eight overs) but not too badly, whereas the 1926 game was, alas, an embarrassment. Northants scored 454 for seven declared and Adams contributed his 87. It was in the University's second innings that things really went awry. They had already lost a wicket in the first over, before the ball was tossed to Adams to bowl at opener Samuel Beckett. Having bowled him first ball for one, he bowled the incoming batsman with his second and, for good measure, took a third wicket in the same over. Six for 32 in seven overs, and the University were out for 58.

Beckett retained an interest in cricket for many years. In the mid 1960s he was on his way to an Ashes Test at Lord's, waxing enthusiastically on the green trees, the birdsong and friendship in general. One friend remarked that it was indeed good to be alive. 'Well, I wouldn't go as far as that,' replied Beckett!

Carr Damaged by Mercutio's Rapier

England v Australia, 3rd Test, Headingley, July 1926

Arthur Carr was an enterprising captain of Nottinghamshire and an outstanding slip who let little go by, round, over or through him. In 1926 England were trying – yet again – to wrest back the Ashes which Australia had held since 1920. Since World War I, England had lost twelve out of fifteen Tests against the old enemy. This year there was a belief that the pendulum was swinging back, and that Carr was the attacking captain needed to recover England's lost glory. The first Test was washed out and the second a high-scoring draw, in which Charlie Macartney, the 'Governor General', made 133. Battle was renewed in the next Test at Headingley.

Carr won the toss and, astonishingly, put Australia in on a dead pitch. Off the very first ball, Maurice Tate had Warren Bardsley, scorer of 193 in the previous Test, caught by Herbert Sutcliffe at first slip. Australia nought for one, the perfect start. In came the Governor General, the man Cardus called 'Mercutio, because he would not fight by the book of arithmetic'. Tate's fifth ball lifted, Macartney flashed at it and it flew to Carr's left at third slip. Carr got both hands to it – and dropped it! He must have known he'd dropped the match as

48

well. George Geary was alongside at the time. Asked for Carr's reaction, he simply commented, 'Unprintable, I'm afraid!'

Luckily for England, Macartney lasted a mere two and a half hours. Unluckily for England, he made 151 in that short time – including a hundred before lunch, just like Trumper 24 years before. It was an innings of dazzling brilliance. 'Thank the Lord Carr dropped that catch, else we'd never have seen this innings!' That, wrote Cardus, was what he heard Englishman after Englishman saying during the interval, and in an Ashes series, there cannot be higher praise than that.

In the end, England escaped from Headingley with a hard-won draw. The fourth Test at Old Trafford was ruined by rain, though not before Macartney had had time for another century, his third in succession. The England selectors decided that not only was Arthur Carr not weather-proof, but he was accident-prone as well, and replaced him with the dashing Percy Chapman, who duly won back the Ashes at the Oval with a massive 289-run victory.

The Hon. F S G Calthorpe Forgets His Slide Rule

West Indies v England, 4th Test, Sabina Park, most of April 1930

No doubt his children loved him dearly but, as skippers go, the Hon. F S G Calthorpe seems to have bumbled more than most (see page 37). Failing anyone better, he was in charge of the first England team to play a Test series in the Caribbean. If the West Indies were short of experienced players, they nevertheless had in George Headley one of the finest batsmen ever to have played, as he demonstrated with three centuries and a double hundred in the four-game series. After three Tests, the series was balanced with a win to each side, and the decision was taken to play the final match to a finish, irrespective of time. The match began on 3 April.

Opening for England, Andy Sandham made 325, the highest individual Test score ever recorded (until Bradman eclipsed it at Headingley three months later). Les Ames became the first wicket-keeper to score a century for England, and the side's final tally was 849. With Headley failing for once, the West Indies reply was a relatively modest 286. Wilfred Rhodes, playing in his last Test almost 32 years after his first appearance as a twenty-year-old in 1899 – the longest-ever Test career – took one for 17.

With a slender lead of 563, Calthorpe pondered one of life's trickier decisions. Should he enforce the follow-on? To universal astonishment, he decided to bat again. 'I suppose,' thought Ames, 'because there were still six clear days before the departure of our ship.' Got to keep the chaps amused, what? England made 272 in their second innings, so West Indies needed only 836 for a rubber-clinching victory.

By the time Headley (223) was out they had reached 408 for five, and as far as anyone could remember about a week had passed. The England players found sleep difficult in the high humidity, so when rain washed out the next two days, they were relieved to board their ship and abandon the first, 'forgotten' Timeless Test. But the Hon. F S G Calthorpe must have felt a bit of a duffer.

Don Dents Percy's Fender

Surrey v Australia,
the Oval, May 1930

Percy Fender, scorer of the fastest century (35 minutes) in first-class cricket, was a shrewd and unorthodox captain of Surrey with a conjuror's array of tricks, any one of which might be pulled from his sleeve without warning. He was also a believer in psychological pressure. Covering England's 1928–9 series in Australia as a reporter, Percy had seen the young Don Bradman at close quarters, and recognised a potent threat to England's prospects when the Aussies visited in 1930. In newspaper articles he attempted to counteract the threat by labelling Bradman 'brilliant but unsound'. He had no intention of boosting Aussie morale by pronouncing him a great player, and forecast that when he played against Surrey early in the tour he would not succeed. According to Queenslander Percy Hornibrook, who was in the team that day at the Oval, Don finished reading one of Fender's articles and said simply 'We'll see.'

Conditions were cold and damp and, Bradman apart, Australia struggled. Even the Don was careful, taking what, for him, was a long ninety minutes to reach fifty, after which he allowed himself the pleasurable luxury of an assault on Fender's bowling. He reached his century in just under two and a half hours, and at tea was unbeaten on 142 out of 240 for five. Thereafter he shredded the bowling, and according to one of his biographers not a single ball went through to the wicket-keeper. 'He finished with 252 not out – with men all over the field,' Hornibrook recalled. 'As he came in one of the boys said to the rest of us, "Don't say a word." Don threw his bat in the corner with the comment: "I wonder what Fender's going to say in the morning's paper?"' The *Observer* wrote the next day, 'Recollection of the innings will always be happy to those privileged to witness it.' Fender wisely kept quiet, though his shrewd observations on Australian weaknesses around the leg stump were later to be expanded into Bodyline theory.

Goliath Put Down For a Count of Nine

Northamptonshire v Australia, August 1930

Between the wars they had little to cheer on the County Ground in Northampton. In Edwardian times, they had started impressively in the County Championship, but after World War I they flirted regularly with bankruptcy, and were usually near the foot of the table. Indeed between 1930 and 1939 they would be bottom no fewer than seven times. The Australians, by contrast, were making huge scores everywhere they played in 1930, with young Don Bradman leading the way. In four Tests so far, he had made 742 runs at an average of 123.66, and as the game against Northants was to be followed by the deciding fifth Test, the Aussies wanted some good batting practice.

In those pre-TV days the coming of the Australians was a great event, and the ground was packed to capacity as the Northants openers put on a hundred in as many minutes, the county finishing with a respectable 249. Next day, Sunday, it rained hard, and when the Australians batted on Monday, the sun came out to make the wicket interesting. Jupp and Thomas, the county bowlers, knew exactly what to do with it.

When Archie Jackson was out at 37, Bradman 'advanced to the wicket amid deafening cheers' according to the *Northampton*

Echo. But he and Woodfull managed only 14 together, and Jupp (six for 32) bowled them both, Bradman for 22. With Thomas taking three for 29 the Aussies were whipped out for 93, their lowest score of the tour. 'Spectators hardly able to believe their eyes,' panted the *Echo*. Subjected to the indignity of following on, Australia ground slowly to 405 for eight and survived. Northants had their hour of glory, and the substantial takings at the gate guaranteed survival of another sort. Australia went on to the Oval, scored 695 (Bradman 232) and won both the Test and the Ashes.

Fate Trips Up the Don

Australia v South Africa, 5th Test, Melbourne, February 1932

The South Africans were sick to death of Bradman by the time they got to Melbourne for the last Test of their 1931–2 tour down under. In four tests so far, his scores had been 226, 112, 2, 167 and 299 not out – an aggregate of 806, average 201.5. In the five-match series against England in 1930, the Don's aggregate had been a record 976 runs. Those knowing Bradman fully expected him to set his sights on another double-century to break his own record, and go on past a thousand runs for the series – a feat not achieved before or since. For good measure, the Don had also thrashed 135 and 219 off the South Africans in a couple of games for New South Wales, so clearly their bowlers needed voodoo or divine intervention on their side.

They got it in spades – and spurned it. The wicket turned out to be a vicious 'sticky', of the kind only Melbourne could produce. Had their prayers been answered? But would it help, since the normal rules of batsmanship seemed not to apply to Bradman? So, on winning the toss, they chose to bat – maybe the wicket would get worse as the match progressed. In the dressing room, the Australians prepared to go out and field. Bradman stood up, caught his studs in the dressing-room mat and strained his ankle ligaments so badly he couldn't even hobble, never mind bat.

How did the South Africans celebrate this gift of the gods? With the lowest-ever Test innings of 36, which they followed with 45 when they had another shot! In between these two pathetic efforts the Australians managed 153 – without Bradman – and won by an innings. The match lasted less than a day, and the aggregate of 234 runs is still the smallest ever for a completed Test.

Arthur Blows It

England v Australia, 1st Test, Trent Bridge, June 1934

Despite the many times they have each been out in the nineties, nobody thinks of Steve Waugh and Michael Slater as chokers. But the label hung round Arthur Chipperfield's neck for the rest of his career, although it happened to him only once.

The 1934 Australians were a formidable team – apart from skipper Bill Woodfull, there was Bill Ponsford, Bill Brown, Stan McCabe, Bill O'Reilly, and Clarrie Grimmett. Not forgetting one D G Bradman. In the party was the uncapped Arthur Chipperfield, and (despite not being called Bill) he was picked for the first Test at Trent Bridge. Between the wars, the Bridge was usually a batsman's wicket, but in this game no-one was destined to post a century. Batting first, Ponsford (53) and McCabe (65) were the notable performers in the top order, but Chipperfield did most to get Australia to their total of 374. Batting at No 7, he reached lunch on the second day with his score on 99. It was not that he had batted with great distinction, hitting the ball uppishly on many occasions, particularly through the off side. Nevertheless, here he was at lunch on the verge of a century in his first Test.

Legend has it that he spent an agonising, chain-smoking forty minutes, pacing the locker room. He remembered it differently: 'Nobody in the dressing room doubted that I would score another single, and it never occurred to me that I would miss a century.' As they went out again after the break, Grimmett warned him to play back against quickie Ken Farnes. But to the third delivery, 'I judged that I could get forward and drive it for the single I needed. Instead I nicked it and wicket-keeper Les Ames caught it . . . so I found myself alone as the only player to make ninety-nine in his first Test.'

Clarrie's Costly Leg Break

Grimmett & Richardson testimonial match, Adelaide Oval, 1937

Leg-spinner Clarrie Grimmett was not one of life's jokers. Unlike Arthur Mailey, his predecessor in the Australian XI, who could see the funny side of anything, Grimmett regarded the art of spinning a ball as too important for levity. Even in his seventies he was still experimenting with new types of delivery. He had a cricket net in the garden, and there he would take visitors. He would mark the spot on which he was going to drop the ball and tell them exactly how much he was going to spin it and which way. No, there was nothing funny about batsmen, even thirty years after he'd retired. They existed to be bowled out and had no other use in life.

Between 1928 and 1935 Clarrie played for Australia 37 times and took 216 wickets, and in 1937 he and Vic Richardson (grandfather of Ian, Greg and Trevor Chappell) were given a joint testimonial match arranged by their state, South Australia. Richardson would captain one side, containing Grimmett, and Don Bradman, who'd recently moved from New South Wales to captain South Australia, would skipper the other. In other words, Clarrie would find himself bowling to Bradman.

According to Richardson, Grimmett had a bit of a bone to pick with Don Bradman. 'Clarrie loved taking wickets because that was his duty and his task,' Richardson would tell people, 'but he loved bowling even more, because the true craftsman loves his craft above all things.' As usual, he was experimenting, thinking up new types of delivery. The previous season, he had become obsessive about bowling a wrong 'un with a flicked finger, and no matter how often his new skipper, Bradman, would ask him to bowl more leg breaks, he couldn't bring himself to abandon his new toy. Bradman finally declared Grimmett no longer able to bowl the leg break. This probably cost him his place in the Australian side – worse, it insulted the pride of a dedicated craftsman.

On the first day of the testimonial match, a Friday, Richardson's side batted first. Since the whole point of the game was to raise as much money as possible for Grimmett's and Richardson's retirement, it was important that Bradman should be batting on Saturday afternoon. If he was at the crease then it was reckoned an additional forty thousand would come to the ground after lunch, when they knocked off work, just to see him.

In the event, the Don came in to bat shortly before lunch on the Saturday. So far, so good. Whatever else happened, he must not be out, and as Grimmett was to bowl the last over before the interval to Bradman, Richardson's mind was, he said, at rest. 'Clarrie could be counted on to realise how his bread was buttered – his bread and my bread.' He should have known him better. The fourth ball pitched on a perfect length just outside leg stump, spun sharply and removed the off bail with surgical precision. 'That'll teach him I can still bowl a leg break,' yelled an exultant Grimmett to Richardson.

Richardson's reply was on the pithy side. According to contemporary accounts, it contained some words which the dictionaries of the day had yet to record, and even Shakespeare might not have recognised. Many years later, when he came to write his account of the incident, he was feeling more temperate about the business, and owned up to saying, 'I suppose you know you've bowled us out of a thousand pounds?' – although we can be reasonably sure that this is merely an approximate summary of the soliloquy that took place. 'Clarrie looked sorry for my sake, but I doubt whether he was for his own. The feat of bowling Bradman with so perfectly pitched a leg break was sufficient reward.'

When Grimmett bowled, he did not think and plan a couple of balls or an over ahead, but sometimes an hour ahead, plotting to draw each batsman inexorably into his trap. He was proud of the fact that, when Bradman was still playing for New South Wales, he averaged twenty less against South Australia than against others. The ball which cost £1,000 may have been a bad joke to Richardson, but it was a perfect one for Clarrie, and without doubt he treasured it for the rest of his life.

Please Play With Us – We'll Bring a Bat and Ball

New Zealand v Australia, Wellington, March 1946

Why did it take over forty years for Australia to crush New Zealand against its hairy cricketing bosom in welcome embrace? They are neighbours, separated only by the Tasman Sea, but for a long time mutual suspicion seemed to colour the current between them. Yet cricket has been played in New Zealand almost as long as in Australia – Charles Darwin saw a game in progress there in 1835. England began playing Test matches against the Kiwis in 1929, South Africa in 1931 and, when India and Pakistan joined the international scene in the years after World War II, they and the West Indies were quick to add New Zealand to their itinerary. An Australian XI did visit the country in March 1946 and, while there, played against the New Zealand team (the match was given Test status later), but it was not until December 1973 that official Test series between the two neighbours were inaugurated.

Perhaps that match in 1946 was part of the problem. New Zealand did themselves few favours in the game, which was over almost before the spectators had unpacked their picnics. They got to 37, with two wickets down, before that mighty veteran of Aussie inter-war triumphs, Bill O'Reilly, started the mayhem. Whether or not it was his considerable presence that unnerved the Kiwis, 37 for two quickly became 37 for seven, and finally 42 all out. O'Reilly had taken five for 14 in 12 overs, and the last eight wickets yielded just five runs, a spectacular collapse by anybody's standards. On grounds of common humanity, they held him back a little in the second innings, but he still bagged three as New Zealand tumbled to 54, losing by an innings and 103. The game had lasted for only eight and a half hours.

It was humiliating, but considering the hiatus caused by World War II, Australia's unwillingness to play New Zealand again for more than a quarter of a century seems harsh. Maybe it contributed to a popular Kiwi insult: 'Every time an Australian goes home, the average IQ of both countries rises!'

Mr Miller Regrets,
He's Unwilling to Bat Today

Keith Miller's famous duck – Essex v Australia, Southend, May 1948

1948 – the year of Bradman's Invincibles. It had been ten years since the last Ashes series to be played in England, and the public looked forward to seeing the new faces in the Australian party – men like Ray Lindwall, Arthur Morris, Bill Johnstone, Don Tallon and the glamorous Keith Miller. During World War II Miller had been a fighter pilot, and in the Victory Tests of 1946 had made his reputation as a formidable fast bowler and dashing middle-order batsman. Like England's Bill Edrich, another wartime flying ace, he knew he was lucky to be alive and was determined to relish every moment of the extended life he'd been granted.

The sixth match of the Australian tour was against Essex at Southend, and Essex distinguished themselves by being the first side to bowl the tourists out. 'The slight snag,' as Trevor Bailey admitted, 'was that they had scored a little matter of 721.' This is still the highest six-hour total ever recorded. Opener Bill Brown made 153 in three hours, and Bradman 187 in 125 minutes. These two had put on 219 for the second wicket before Brown was out with the score on 364. Miller came to the wicket, took a perfunctory guard, lifted his bat to let the ball hit the stumps, and was on his way back to the pavilion before the bails had hit the ground. At the other end, Bradman remarked to Bailey, the bowler, 'He'll learn,' but he never did. Keith Miller relished a worthy challenge, but was just not interested in feasting on easy pickings. The idea had no appeal for him.

This didn't prevent the incident becoming the stuff of legends. One theory had it that Bradman had met him in his dinner jacket at breakfast time, returning from his night's entertainment, and batting up the order was his punishment. But the story best fitting Miller's habits and personality is that he was enjoying a winning streak at cards in the pavilion and wanted to get back before his luck changed. With Keith Miller, prince of cricketers, you could never be sure!

England Snatch Defeat From the Jaws of Victory

England v Australia, 4th Test, Headingley, July 1948

Bradman's Invincibles have been labelled the greatest Australian team of all time. Maybe they were, but because we have since become accustomed to weak English performances it would be a mistake to think the England team of 1948 provided unworthy opposition. Compton with the bat, and Bedser with the ball were especially heroic, and while the series was in the balance it was only in the second Test at Lord's that England could be said to have been outplayed. The first Test was within a whisker of being drawn, and England were well on top when the third was ruined by rain, so when the fourth Test began England still had some hopes of squaring the series.

Hutton (81) and Washbrook (143) put on 168 for the first wicket before Edrich (111) and Washbrook took the score to 268. Alec Bedser (79), coming in as night watchman, then helped Edrich to add another 155 to take the score to 423 before the third wicket fell. It was at this point that a modern failing overtook England, the middle order collapsed, and they were all out for 496. In their turn, Australia batted none too well to begin with, and when Bradman was bowled by Pollard they were 68 for three. At this critical point Keith Miller, in

John Arlott's words, 'played like an emperor'. Teenager Neil Harvey, in his first Ashes Test, was in trouble against Laker, so Miller took the strike, hit Laker's first ball to him for six, and with a string of daring strokes, seized the initiative from England. Miller eventually went for 58. 'It was not merely a great innings,' wrote Arlott, 'but I cannot believe it possible for a cricket brain to conceive of any innings which could be greater.' Harvey, now well set, went on to score 112, and with a rollicking 93 from Sam Loxton, Australia closed on 458, giving England a lead of 38.

England scored consistently right down the order in their second innings, reaching the morning of the last day with a lead of 400 and two wickets in hand. They batted on for two overs before declaring, in order to use the heavy roller to further break up what had already become a leg-spinner's wicket. This was a brilliant idea but for the fact that England weren't playing a regular leggie. Doug Wright was out through injury, and although Jack Young had been in the twelve for this game, he had then been left out. Now they must rely on Compton's chinaman, which could be unpredictable, and on Jim Laker who was an off-spinner. Nevertheless, Bradman was so certain Australia would lose that he ordered the team coach to be ready at three-thirty.

As befitted a side convinced it was on a hiding, Australia started with great caution. Laker and Compton were brought into the attack and, almost immediately, Compton dismissed Hassett. It was then that it all began to go horribly wrong. Laker simply could not control his length, and it was left to Compton to pose the problems. His chinamen may have been unpredictable, but before lunch on that fifth day they were brilliant. Not only did he tie the batsmen, Morris and Bradman, in knots but, unfortunately for England, he baffled the fielders too. Godfrey Evans, normally the surest of keepers, missed stumping Morris when he had 32. Bradman was dropped at slip off Compton before lunch, and again when he was 59. Shortly before the break, skipper Norman Yardley gambled by calling up the gentle, occasional leg spin of Len Hutton. The gamble failed. Morris and Bradman hit five consecutive fours and the whole tempo of the innings changed. Bradman said later it was at this point that he realised it was easier to win than to hang on for a draw.

Courtesy of more missed catches and another missed stumping, Australia reached the largest fourth innings total in Ashes history to win by seven wickets. Morris scored 182, and Bradman 173 not out. 'We were all so delighted at being on top when Australia batted that we never got down to solid concentration,' said Godfrey Evans later. 'We lost – and we should have won.'

Three Cheers for the Don

Bradman's last Test innings
England v Australia, the Oval, August 1948

The Oval, 14 August 1948. Don Bradman, the greatest batsman the world has seen, needed just four runs to end his Test career with an average of one hundred. A little before six o'clock at the end of the first day, he came down the pavilion steps to a tumultuous reception from the capacity crowd. England had already been shot out for a paltry 52, Lindwall taking six for 20, and in reply Australia had just lost their first wicket with the score on 117. The stage was set. The wicket was good. Australia already had a lead, and over the years the Oval had seen some of the Don's greatest innings.

Norman Yardley shook Bradman's hand and called for three cheers, then all was ready. Bradman scratched out his guard with his boot, and settled to face leg-spinner Eric Hollies. The first ball pitched on an immaculate length, whipped past bat and off stump through to Godfrey Evans behind the wicket. The second ball dropped on exactly the same spot, but this time it was the googly, turning the other way. Bradman didn't spot it and stretched for the leg break, but it turned inside the bat and hit the off stump. Bradman looked round at his wicket. Just for a moment, he couldn't believe it. But it had happened, and with a half-smile he turned and began the long walk back. For a few seconds the crowd was silent, amazed by what had happened, but then the cheering followed him into the pavilion.

Had Bradman's nerve failed? Had there been tears in his eyes affecting his judgement? Had he, most unpardonable of thoughts, allowed a moist-eyed clanger to fall? You might as well ask if Churchill lost his nerve in World War II. The Don always denied he was affected by the warmth of his send-off, and those around him at the time agreed – with one exception. From behind the stumps, Evans – maybe writing later what a sentimental public wanted to believe – claimed to have suspected a moist eye, though he admitted, 'the ball which bowled him might have got anybody.'

England's Young Hopefuls in a Tailspin

England v The Rest, Test trial, Bradford, May 1950

Test trials were briefly in vogue around the middle of the twentieth century, and prior to the visit of the West Indies in 1950 one such trial was scheduled for Bradford, starting (and very nearly finishing) on a chilly day before a scattering of hardy spectators. On the scorecard for The Rest were such names as David Sheppard, Peter May, Don Kenyon, Freddie Trueman and Les Jackson.

Jim Laker was blamed for England's failure to beat Australia in the fourth Test of 1948 (see page 67), and had won only one cap since. Nevertheless, he was in the England side that day, and when he saw the wet wicket drying in the stiff breeze, he must have seen an England recall beckoning. After a nominal twenty minutes of seam, enough to claim Sheppard's wicket, the ball was tossed to Laker. As John Arlott described: 'He strolled back to his mark at his characteristic constabulary gait, then jogged the approach he used artfully to vary, to defeat the batsman's timing.' The young England hopefuls pushed forward defensively, but it was inadequate against the spiteful leap and turn of the ball. Doggart (2) and May (0) were caught close to the wicket in Laker's first over; Carr (0) and Kenyon (7) followed soon after, and still not a run had been scored off him when Laker's Surrey colleague, Eric Bedser, came in. Brother Alec at mid-off moved back a few yards, Laker sent down a full toss and Eric had his single to get off the mark. That was the end of charity.

Ninety minutes after Laker had come on, The Rest were taking a miserable early lunch after making 27, the smallest-ever score in a representative match. If the selectors had noticed them, it was hardly for the best of reasons. Jim Laker probably washed down his lettuce leaf with something celebratory, but it did him little good. Despite an analysis of 14 overs, 12 maidens, eight for two, he was called up by England for only three games in the next four Test series. His hour of greatest glory, when he took 19 wickets in a Test against Australia (see page 88), still lay six years in the future.

Death or Glory
for the Barnacle

Essex v Lancashire,
Brentwood, June 1952

Consider Trevor Bailey, Essex and England, soon to become celebrated as Barnacle Bailey, occupier of the crease in a crisis, real or imaginary. In six years' time, he will score the then slowest Test match half-century, an 'outrageous display' taking seven and a half hours for 68 in the first Test against Australia in Brisbane. Further into the future, when he has stopped playing, he will become a radio and TV guru, and author of books on how to play cricket. 'The one thing a batsman must avoid,' he will write, forgetful of a June day at Brentwood in 1952, 'is losing his head. He must avoid having a death-or-glory swing.'

It was the second game of the 1952 Brentwood week. The first had been against Leicestershire, and Essex had chased 195 at two runs a minute to win by a couple of wickets with a single ball remaining. The Essex side of those days enjoyed their cricket, and didn't need urging to play entertainingly. It was what came naturally to them, though that in no way dimmed their pleasure in winning the *News Chronicle* Trophy for Brighter Cricket in this, its inaugural year.

Brian Statham's Lancashire, the visitors for the second game of the festival, made heavy weather of their first innings, batting, the *Manchester Guardian* reported, 'for long periods of the day as though they suspected both bowlers and the wicket of being possessed of some hidden venom.' In reply to Lancashire's 266, Essex made an excellent start, but then faltered and, despite Bailey giving a preview of his later reputation by batting most of the second morning for 34, it was thanks to a vigorous 56 by tail-ender Bill Greensmith that they finished on 261, conceding a first-innings lead of only five, as the third and final day began.

In those far-off days, the winning side took twelve points and, in a drawn game, four points went to the side with the first-innings lead. The loser took nothing. If the game finished as a tie, four points were awarded to each team. Essex, therefore, had every incentive to win, while if Lancashire chose to settle just for their four first-innings points they could shut the game up. This thought was furthest from Lancastrian minds as they sprinted to a declaration score of 226 for seven in three and a quarter hours, leaving Essex 232 for victory in 140 minutes.

With twelve points to gain and none to lose, there was no question of Essex declining the challenge, and it wasn't in their natures to do so. Doug Insole promoted himself to open with Dickie Dodds, of whose batting he once said, 'It's fit for a World Eleven or the madhouse.' Bailey was lowered to No 8. Statham, that peerlessly accurate England fast bowler, came gliding in. Dodds pulled his first ball for four, hooked his second over the beer tent for six and walloped another six in Statham's second over. It didn't last – how could it – but after 25 minutes Essex were 50 for two; after 50 minutes, 100 for four; and when their fifth wicket went after eighty minutes, the score was 150. Bailey came in with 75 still needed in less than an hour. Wickets continued to fall.

Frank Vigar had twelve first-class centuries to his name but, not being a hitter, he was No 11 in a run chase. He joined Bailey with 26 still required, and together they whittled the target down to nine as the last over began. To Malcolm Hilton's first ball, Bailey played an immaculate forward defensive shot. Groans all round the ground. The second ball seemed identical but, picking the longest boundary, Bailey off-drove it for six. Three runs wanted, four balls left. Bailey repeated the shot next ball, but didn't middle it. According to the *Brentwood Gazette*: 'Wharton, running hard round the pavilion rails, took the ball waist high but could not hold it,' while the batsmen galloped two. The scores were level. Three deliveries left to nudge a single and scoop all twelve points. As the pundit was to write, one must avoid death-or-glory swings, so what does he do with the fourth ball? Goes for another off-driven six! Two thousand spectators leapt to their feet with a 'yell that must have reverberated throughout the country'. But he hadn't middled it and was brilliantly caught at long-off. Match tied – Essex 4 points; Lancashire 8.

'Right,' Said Fred, 'Line and Length'

England v India, 1st Test, Headingley, June 1952

We all know that 'Fiery Fred' Trueman was one of Test history's greatest fast bowlers and, to ensure you hadn't overlooked it, he's reminded us of it frequently. Line and length, length and line. How often on *Test Match Special* Fred bemoaned its absence. But, as Frankie Howerd might have said, titter ye not until you've considered his sensational Test debut.

The unfortunate victims were India. Only four months earlier, in Madras, they had gained their first Test victory over England, but on the 1952 tour their approach was largely defensive and, as Wisden said, 'this proved useless against the battering rams of Bedser and Trueman'.

In the first Test, India had surrendered a narrow first-innings lead of 41 to England. Within a few minutes of their second innings, the deficit was still 41, but now they had only six wickets remaining. The scoreboard read an amazing – and unparalleled – nought for four. Bedser had one of them, and Fred the other three, two clean bowled and one caught in the slips. 'The Indians had not encountered anything like me,' wrote Fred, and who could argue? As often happens to a side subjected to sustained, hostile bowling, India's confidence progressively weakened against Trueman's unrelenting speed and accuracy.

The lowest point came in the third Test, when they were dismissed twice in a single day, for 58 and 82. Bedser took a wicket with the sixth ball of their first innings. 'Right,' thought Fred, 'there's still nine of 'em left,' and set about getting them in short order as the Indian batsmen began to panic. 'When I knocked over Polly Umrigar's stumps, one bail broke and pieces of it carried to just short of the boundary,' he recorded. He finished the innings with eight for 31, and the four-match series with 29 wickets. Of these, 16 were clean bowled, and most of the rest caught at slip or backward short leg. You can't argue with that for line and length. The Indians certainly didn't.

Did This Catch Spill the Ashes Crown?

England v Australia, 2nd Test, Lord's, June 1953

Coronation Year. Elizabeth II had been safely crowned three weeks before, as news broke of Hillary and Tenzing's conquest of Everest. There was much media talk of a new Elizabethan age, but would it spread to the cricket field? For nineteen long years the Ashes had been buttoned away in the Wallaby pouch but this year, surely, England could compete on level terms? Expectation was in the air as the Coronation Ashes series began. The first Test was grimly contested, but rain washed away any chance of a result. At Lord's, no side appeared to be gaining the upper hand – until the last hour of the fourth day. Australia had made 346 in their first innings (Hassett 104), and England had taken a slight lead with a reply of 372 (Hutton 145). Australia answered with 368 and so, as the England openers made their way to the middle on the fourth evening, their target for victory was 343. For a few fleeting moments, as the nation pressed its collective ear to the wireless set, optimism held sway, only to vanish like smoke in the wind. Ray Lindwall, a hard-hitting 50 already behind him, was to be hero and villain within the hour. His opening spell was devastating, dismissing both openers by the time the score had reached 10, and at the other end wicket-keeper Gil Langley took a thrilling diving catch to dismiss Graveney to make it 12 for three. Enter Willie Watson to join Dennis Compton. Thoughts of victory were gone. Survival was the only objective, and even that seemed distant. Doug Ring was brought on, and almost immediately Watson turned him into the hands of Lindwall at backward short leg – and was dropped!

Next day, in what David Frith called 'one of the most celebrated of match-saving stands', Watson (109) and Trevor Bailey (71) batted virtually all day as the nation held its breath. Their partnership of 163 saved England, who went on to recapture the Ashes at the Oval.

The Day the Vanquished Wouldn't Submit

South Africa v New Zealand, 2nd Test, Johannesburg, December 1953

Strictly speaking, this chapter doesn't belong in a book on cricket clangers. The pretext for it is that on the second day of the game, which was also Boxing Day 1953, New Zealand were reduced to a shambles, only to be rescued by a display of astonishing bravery that won the hearts of the tough Springbok spectators, and had many of them weeping openly. The only clanging heard was the sound of ball hitting head.

This was the first time New Zealand had toured South Africa. They had lost the first Test by an innings, and here in Johannesburg had reduced the home side to 259 for eight on the first day, Christmas Eve. Before play began on Boxing Day word came in of a dreadful rail crash in New Zealand, with heavy loss of life including the fiancée of opening bowler Bob Blair. Blair stayed behind in the team's hotel when his colleagues left for the ground to resume play. The Springbok innings was quickly wrapped up for 271 – a prelude, it seemed in retrospect, to a day of almost unimaginable drama.

The pitch was thoroughly spiteful and Neil Adcock, one of the fastest bowlers of the day, produced, according to Wisden, 'one of Test cricket's most lethal spells'. This came close to the literal truth. Opener Murray Chapple was bowled off his chest, and the score was nine for two when that prince of left-handers, Bert Sutcliffe, came to the wicket. New Zealand cricket writer Dick Brittenden described what happened as the third ball flew off a length: 'Sutcliffe was hit on the left ear, and the ambulance men ran out... He went to hospital and collapsed twice during treatment. There was an announcement that he would be unable to bat again.' John Reid was hit five sickening blows while making three in 25 minutes, and Lawrie Miller left the field coughing blood after being hit. At lunch, New Zealand were 41 for four with two men retired hurt. Miller returned when the fifth wicket fell and he battled on to take the score to 82 before going for 14. Then, to everyone's astonishment, Sutcliffe emerged, ashen-faced, his head swathed in a turban of bandages. He was applauded all the way to the wicket by crowd and players alike. The third ball he'd received before lunch had half-killed him. At this second attempt, he had a different fate in mind for the third ball, despatching it for six, and followed this with two more sixes at the other end. 'Graceful violence' Dick Brettenden called it as, with Frank Mooney, he added 50 in 33 minutes. It couldn't be expected to last on that wicket and, when Mooney (35) was seventh out, the tail quickly surrendered, leaving Sutcliffe unbeaten in the fifties.

At 154 for nine, with Bob Blair back in the hotel, as they thought, the players began to move towards the pavilion. 'Then there was a sudden, almost chilling silence, giving a dramatic day its most poignant moment.' There on the pavilion steps, putting on his gloves, was Bob Blair. The South Africans stood still. Sutcliffe went to meet him, put his arm round him, and together they walked slowly to the wicket, Blair brushing the tears away with the back of his glove. Every single person in the crowd stood in absolute silence. And then the mayhem began. Sutcliffe hit another 27 in nine minutes, including three sixes in four balls before taking a single to leave three balls for his partner. Refusing to be denied his part in the drama, Blair hit the second for six before being stumped. The gallant pair had put on 33 in ten minutes, and taken New Zealand's score to 187, a truly heroic performance on such an appalling wicket. Sutcliffe, who had been declared unfit to bat, had hit seven sixes and four fours in making 80 not out in ninety minutes.

In a fairy story, New Zealand would have gone on to win. They did well with their less powerful attack to put South Africa out for 148 in their second innings, but could muster only 100 in their own second attempt, Adcock taking five more wickets, and went down by 132 runs. Bob Blair returned to New Zealand for three weeks, but was back in time to play in the fourth Test a month later.

The Lindwall Bouncer
That Bounced Back

Australia v England, 2nd Test,
Sydney, December 1954

England's Frank Tyson was fast – very fast indeed. In his 1952 debut match at Northampton, three slips were posted and, being warned he was on the quick side, stood well back. Tyson's third ball took the bat's edge and struck first slip Fred Jakeman's kneecap with a crack (and a yell from Fred) that might have been heard in Wellingborough. After five minutes he was upright again, and all three slips carefully retreated several more yards.

Having regained the Ashes in 1953, Len Hutton took a blend of youth (including Tyson) and experience to defend the Ashes in Australia in the winter of 1954–5. The first Test in Brisbane was unrelieved disaster. Hutton put Australia in, they scored 601, fourteen catches were dropped, Compton broke his hand fielding, and Tyson took one for 160 in just 29 overs. England lost by an innings, but Hutton kept faith with his speed attack and retained it for the second Test.

In Sydney, England batted first, and poorly, making only 154, then conceded a lead of 74 to Australia, Tyson taking four middle-order wickets. He came in to bat in England's second innings with the score at 222 for five. The great Ray Lindwall was bowling and, although he was approaching the end of his war-shortened career, was still distinctly fast, and with a well-disguised bouncer. He bowled it now, straight and lethal. Tyson turned his back on it, it hit him on the head and he collapsed, having to be helped off the field. Onlookers were convinced it was the end of his match and were astonished when, at the fall of the next wicket, he reappeared, bat in hand. Lindwall soon bowled him, for nine, perhaps reflecting that the bouncer had done its work and set Tyson up for the full-length delivery later. If so, he had little idea how heavy a penalty Tyson was going to extract for that perfect bouncer!

Coming on first change in Australia's second innings, Tyson shortened his run. A legend grew that he was still feeling the effects of the blow on his head, but Tyson himself insisted that he had merely reverted to the shorter run of his early years, concentrating everything into his delivery stride, controlling his accuracy without sacrificing his speed. Whatever the reason, the results were spectacular. He took six for 85, as the Aussies fell 38 runs short of a modest target, and England squared the series.

Tyson's ferocious speed in Sydney had given Australia a shock, but it was at Melbourne in the third Test that the Australian batting capitulated in the face of it.

England batted first on a damp pitch and, with Keith Miller returning regal figures of three wickets for five runs before lunch, were only saved from humiliation by the young Colin Cowdrey's finest innings – 102 of an all-out total of 191. Australia gained a first-innings lead of 40, and on an easing pitch England scored 279 in their second effort, leaving Australia to get 240 for victory. By the close of the fourth day, they were 75 for two.

On the final day, 60,000 people brought their picnic lunches to the MCG to enjoy Australia's cruise to victory. The weather forecast made no mention of anything untoward but, towards the end of the morning, a typhoon was to strike and ruin

60,000 picnics. Bowling, as David Frith described, 'at devilish speed', Tyson needed just 51 deliveries to demolish the Australian batting as it suffered a collective loss of nerve. Evans started the procession with a spectacular leg-side catch to dismiss Neil Harvey off Tyson. 'After that catch and the heart it put into the whole side,' said Tyson, 'I never doubted for one moment that we should bowl them out.' Eight wickets went down for just 34 runs and Tyson finished with seven for 27 as Australia were blown away for 111, unlucky 'Nelson', just as they were to be in the second innings of the fourth Test in Adelaide, where England clinched the series and retained the Ashes. Tyson, the tabby cat of Brisbane, had grown into a man-eater, and was known ever after as 'Typhoon'.

Was another England fast bowler, Devon Malcolm, fed on tales of the Lindwall bouncer at his mother's knee? In the third Test against South Africa at the Oval in 1994, Fanie de Villiers hit Devon, a genuine No 11, between the eyes with his first ball. 'You guys are going to pay for this,' he's alleged to have advised anyone within earshot, though sadly the comment is a myth that was invented afterwards. Malcolm's figures of one for 81 in the Springbok first innings hardly suggested menace, but the second innings was a different story. Bowling at top speed with real hostility, Malcolm blazed through the South African batting, creating visible fear and taking nine for 57 to carry England to a spectacular victory.

'The Funniest Thing Since the Marx Brothers'

England v Australia, 4th Test, Old Trafford, July 1956

Those old enough to remember Ken McKay, or 'Slasher' as he was affectionately known, do so with a fond smile and a shake of the head. He had a batting style, and an approach to life, that was unique, and he endeared himself to many during Australia's 1956 and 1961 tours to England. He was as superstitious as they come. The left sock, glove, boot and pad always had to be put on before their right-side counterparts and, as a skipper, he would always toss the coin with his left hand. When he came to write his autobiography there was no chapter 13, and the brand of chewing gum he was never without was, he claimed, a special lucky kind.

He walked out to bat with a rolling gait that John Arlott called his Groucho Marx walk, and at the crease his unorthodox shots defied description – but his marvellous reflexes and big match temperament made them highly effective. 'McKay is like the common cold,' the *Manchester Guardian* wrote. 'There is no known cure for either.'

His tour of England in 1956, though, was none too successful with the bat, and its low point (as for the Australians in general) was the Old Trafford Test – the one celebrated for Laker's 19 wickets. In their two innings, the Aussies recorded eight ducks, and two of them were Slasher's very own to keep. He hit on a plan so cunning that Baldrick would have relished it. He would use his bat only if the ball was in line with the stumps; otherwise, he'd just let it hit him. 'He defended his stumps with every part of his body, the pads, elbows, hands, knees and even his backside. The funniest thing since the Marx Brothers,' said Cardus. 'The first time he attempted to use his bat he got out.' Dear old Slasher. We loved him just the same.

Hanif Runs Out of Puff

Karachi v Bahawalpur, Quaid-e-Azam Trophy
semi-final, January 1959

We've all done it. Gone for a dodgy second run, confident we'll beat the throw. But Brian Lara is the only first-class cricketer who *could* have done it with his score on 498, apart from one other man.

Hanif Mohammed was the most capped (55) of four cricketing brothers (Mushtaq, Wazir and Sadiq being the others) who all played for Pakistan. When he was still seventeen, Hanif played in Pakistan's very first Test, against India in October 1952, and before long was established as an immovable opening bat. He seemed to combine the virtues of skill and inexhaustible patience, exemplified by his 337 against the West Indies in January 1958. With Pakistan following on 473 in arrears, Hanif batted for 16 hours 10 minutes, still the longest innings in Test history.

By contrast, his massive innings for Karachi against Bahawalpur a year later streaked along at 47 runs an hour, and was described by Wisden's Pakistan correspondent as 'a truly brilliant display of stylish hitting'. On the first day, Bahawalpur had been whistled out for 185, allowing Hanif to reach 25 that evening. In five hours on the second day he added 230, and as the third day neared its end he'd amassed a further 244. He'd long since smashed the world's highest score, but a round 500 would be nice by the close. At the other end was a nineteen-year-old rookie, wicket-keeper Abdul Aziz, and when, off the last ball of the day, Hanif called him for a dodgy second to post the magic number, he could hardly yell, 'Stay, skipper! Get back!' could he? So he went, and heard the awful rattle which told him the great man had run himself out on 499!

There's an even sadder end to the story. The Trophy Final took place a few days later. Abdul Aziz was standing up to off-spinner Dildar Awan, and was struck over the heart. He collapsed, and died fifteen minutes later on the way to hospital.

'Whatever You Do, Don't Listen to Godfrey!'

Authors v Publishers, Vincent Square, London, July 1962

Forty years ago, I played for the Publishers in their annual Authors v Publishers fixture. Thanks in part to the great Godfrey Evans, who was turning out for the Authors having retired from his mischievous reign as England and Kent stumper, I was not asked again, though I'm proud to recall that my pads, at least, achieved fifteen minutes of fame. Aidan Crawley, an MP who had just crossed the floor to the opposition benches, opened the Authors' batting. He borrowed my pads, in which he was much photographed for the papers next day and, by a quirk of fate, when he died a great many years later the same photograph was used for his obituary in the *Guardian*.

The game opened in a scotch mist. My pads got a leg bye off the last ball of the first over, and the second was a maiden, which gave Jim Swanton, Crawley's fellow opener, the bowling. Advancing down the wicket with outstretched hand, Jim announced magisterially, 'I'm getting wet. I'm going off' – on which cue Dennis Compton heard the call of the racecourse and disappeared to Ascot. The Publishers' bowlers affected disappointment.

A callow youth waiting to bat, I received plentiful warnings about the disarming bonhomie with which Godfrey Evans could talk out new arrivals at the wicket. Alan Ross, poet, cricket writer and very reasonable medium-pacer, was bowling. I cover drove the second or third ball, an overpitched away swinger, for four. 'Great shot,' said Godfrey, starting to spin the web. 'That's how to play him.' Next over, I repeated the shot. 'Wonderful,' said Godfrey. 'You've got him worked out. Just keep driving him.' So I did, to the very next ball, which wasn't overpitched and wasn't swinging. 'What bad luck,' said Godfrey as he replaced the bails. 'I really thought you were going to make a score there!' I still feel privileged to have been dismissed by such a loveable character.

Siegfried Sassoon's Last (Well, Almost) Match

The Ravens v Mells, Downside School, probably sometime in 1962

The great war poet Siegfried Sassoon grew up loving cricket (see *Memoirs of a Fox-hunting Man*) and, despite the horrors he had endured in World War I, never lost his innocent love of the game. In his mind, he was probably reliving the great days of Frank Woolley and his other Kentish heroes. He lovingly maintained his own cricket ground at Heytesbury House in Wiltshire on which, in his eccentric style, he would unintentionally run out many a bewildered villager by turning up uninvited in the other batsman's crease. His fielding, always at mid-on, was described as 'appalling but of immense courage'. The method never varied. However hard the ball was struck, he would draw himself to attention in its path, and allow it to strike his shins before stooping to retrieve it and lob it underarm to the bowler.

He also turned out from time to time for the Ravens, a side assembled, with enthusiasm and flair, by Father Martin at nearby Downside College, and the last recorded sighting of Sassoon the cricketer was in the Ravens' annual game with Mells, when he was 77. He was, as Dennis Silk recalled, 'tucked discreetly into the late middle order, and there was a corporate ploy of stealth to give him a valedictory lift towards the elusive double figures.' Mells found their slowest bowler of least distinction. The first four full tosses were played with rigid correctness but the fifth, alas, was fatal. Sassoon attempted to hit it for six over the bowler's head and, even in the special circumstances of the day, mid-off could not be expected to drop the embarrassingly easy dolly that resulted. As Sassoon walked off, snorting gently to himself, he was heard to say to no-one in particular, 'The bowling was not worthy of me.' He died five years later.

'There Were Boos and Screams'

Kent v Sussex, 1st round Gillette Cup, Tunbridge Wells, May 1963

Despite the customary protests of those who dislike change of any kind, back in the 1960s cricket badly needed extra money to keep the game alive, and a one-day knockout competition, sponsored by Gillette, was introduced. Although most county captains decided in advance that spinners would not be necessary (their views soon changed), few had stopped to work out the implications of rationing each side, and each bowler, to a given number of overs. They had yet to understand that in this type of cricket, the key is to stop the other side scoring. Ted Dexter, captain of Sussex and England, was the exception.

In the first round of the new competition, Sussex were drawn away to Colin Cowdrey's Kent. Cowdrey attacked, with slips and gully throughout, and made no compromises as Ken Suttle (104) led Sussex on a charge to 314 for seven in the 65 overs then permitted. Kent made a bad start, but at 19 for two Peter Richardson and Cowdrey (31) were threatening to put things right as they added 80 together. Richardson (127) was proving the particular danger man, so Dexter brought new tactics into play. 'It was not my intention to get him out. I set the field back, allowed him to take a single, then bowled tight to the other batsmen. There were boos and screams, and everyone thought it was a rotten thing to do, but there it was. I had shown people what they could be let in for!'

Kent were out for 242, with nine of their allotted overs still unused. Sussex went on to win the first Gillette Final at Lord's, and repeated the trick in 1964. Dexter's approach was criticised, but he had demonstrated how opposing captains could lose if they failed to give adequate thought to every aspect of the game and, of course, the rest soon revised their tactics.

How Are The Mighty Fallen!

Holland wallop Australia, 1964;
Ireland embarrass the Windies, 1969

It's fun to see the big names brought down to earth from time to time. It's what gives football's FA Cup such appeal. When Australia and the West Indies were unexpectedly laid low in the 1960s, cricket's one-day knockout tournament was in its infancy, and in any case the occasional minor-county victory over senior opposition doesn't have quite the same breathtaking appeal as, say, York City bundling out Arsenal in the third round. But to see these international cricketing giants being shown a thing or two, that was different.

When the Aussies ambled across the Channel in late August 1964, they had beaten England 1–0 in the Test series and very satisfactorily retained the Ashes. Now they were on their way to a light-hearted exhibition match against a country that didn't really know much about cricket – or so they may have thought. That was their first mistake. A few years later I was in a bar in Amsterdam asking my English colleague if he'd happened to hear how my county had got on in the championship that day. A Dutchman at the bar leaned across and told me the exact close of play score with details of who'd taken the wickets and made the runs. A lot of the Dutch know a lot about cricket.

Mistake number two was to partake too well of the lavish hospitality on offer, and mistake number three was to assume it would be a quiet match on an out-of-the-way field. It wasn't. There were more than 15,000 spectators (not many fewer than Lord's held at that time) when the Aussies went out to bat on a matting wicket over concrete – 'similar to the surfaces many of us had begun on,' Norman O'Neill admitted later. So no excuses on that score. 'The game looked a pushover,' said Norm. Dear, oh dear! Still, he at least batted respectably and made 87. The trouble was nobody else did. Even the mighty Peter Burge only just scraped past 20 as Australia tottered to 197. Trijzelaar (three for 41) and Pierhagen (three for 75) may be dandling their grandchildren on their knees as you read this, and giving them ball-by-ball commentary on their bowling feats that day.

Even now the Aussies weren't too bothered, but by the time the opening partnership of Marseille and van de Vegt had rattled up 99, doubts were setting in. 'I can assure you we tried our hardest to win against a side in which enthusiasm dwarfed technique,' said one of them, and with 20 needed off the last two overs Australia were still in with a chance of avoiding defeat, at least. They had reckoned without Onstein. Six, four, six and Holland were home by three wickets. 'I remember,' said O'Neill, 'looking round at the disbelief of my team-mates as Onstein clubbed Bob Cowper right out of the ground.' If Dutch hospitality had been lavish during the day it was as nothing to the celebrations that night!

If the West Indies team that went to Dublin in July 1969 was not the fearsome outfit it was to become a decade later, Comacho, Carew, Foster, Butcher, Lloyd, Walcott and Shepherd were not exactly innocents abroad. Between them they could boast an impressive number of Test centuries, and more were to come. So when they won the toss, it was only gracious to bat first and display the batting skills they had brought over from a high scoring draw in the Lord's Test, was it not?

It seems no-one pointed out the wicket's distinctly emerald tinge of green. This would make for slow scoring, as indeed it did. Opening bowlers O'Riordan and Goodwin were forced to toil on it for 25.3 overs while West Indies raced along at fractionally under one an over on their way to an all-out total of 25. Mind you, it could have been worse. The Windies had been twelve for nine! O'Riordan, with four for 18 and Goodwin, with five for six, have probably never enjoyed the black stuff as much as they must have done that night. Just for the record, Ireland passed the Windies total for the loss of only one wicket and entertained the crowd by batting on to 125 for eight before declaring – just to rub the wound a bit harder!

Sensation –
Man Bowled by Bird!

South Australia v Western Australia, Adelaide, November 1969

It was about 5.30 p.m. on the second day, the pitch was true and the light perfect as John Inverarity went out to bat for Western Australia in their second innings. His side was three for one and he'd failed in the first innings, so now he had to stay there till the close. No need to worry about runs, they'd come in the morning. Just avoid risk. For ten minutes he played himself in carefully against Greg Chappell's tidy but innocuous medium-pacers. Then down came a long hop, well wide of the off stump. Inverarity shaped to square cut and gave his stroke the full swing of the bat. He felt nothing, but heard the death rattle behind him as the bails leapt in the air. He turned for the pavilion feeling, he said later, 'finished as a cricketer. If I could make such an awful misjudgement and fail so badly, I had best try no more.'

He'd only taken a few steps when South Australian wicket-keeper, Rex Blundell, dangling a dead swallow by its legs shouted, 'You've killed the bird, you rotten swine! You missed the off stump with it by a foot, and I had to take it on the half-volley!' Swallows often gather at the Adelaide Oval in the early evening, hunting for insects. As Greg Chappell's long hop pitched, a swallow had flashed low across the wicket straight into the path of the ball. The speed of the swallow and the force of the impact had shot the ball off line and into the middle stump.

Inverarity was recalled by the umpires and, revoking his determination to retire, he scored 89 the next day. The umpires' verdict was to declare Chappell's long hop a dead ball, though we can only wonder if the bird thought this a good decision.

Wanted: Volunteers to Look Stupid in the Slips

England v Australia, 1st Test, Old Trafford, June 1972

After losing the 1970–1 Ashes series to Ray Illingworth's side down under, Australia came looking for revenge in 1972. England did their best to oblige in the first Test by selecting a team without specialist slip fielders, despite having John Snow and Geoff Arnold to open the bowling. Later, Tony Greig was to make himself outstanding in this position, and take 87 catches in Tests, but at this point he'd only tried the slips on an occasional basis for Sussex. Nevertheless, Illingworth ordered him to first slip. Lacking further inspiration, he demanded volunteers and up went the hand of that fine fast bowler and outfielder, John Snow. Since beggars can't be choosers, the skipper accepted Snow's generosity. He was not destined to reflect on the decision with satisfaction.

Australia batted first in conditions ideal for swing bowling, and Arnold was just the man for the job. Placing himself at third slip, Illingworth had a grandstand view of the disaster about to unfold as the score stuttered to fourteen without loss. Keith Stackpole was one of Australia's more obdurate openers, but Arnold found an edge and the ball homed in on Snow's head. In what one observer described as 'a flurry of arms and hair' Snow managed only to palm it to the third-man boundary. The next ball Stackpole steered straight to Greig at little more than waist height. He juggled for a moment, and floored it. Having tested the head and the waist, the next ball was guided with some venom onto Snow's foot. The unfortunate Snow, at Illingworth's irate insistence, hopped off back to the outfield and was seen no more at slip.

In theory, England should then have been put to the sword. In fact, they dismissed Australia for 142 and went on to a comfortable victory (though not before Illingworth himself had dropped another slip catch). Three dropped slip catches in successive balls may well constitute a world record, but I wouldn't risk the observation if you find yourself in Geoff Arnold's neighbourhood.

One Wheel On My Wagon, and I'm Still Rolling Along

England v New Zealand, 2nd Test, Lord's, June 1973

Geoff Arnold and dropped catches seemed to go together for a while. Having suffered the bowler's equivalent of martyrdom at Old Trafford a year before, he now found himself the beneficiary at Lord's. England made a poor fist of their first innings (253) against a New Zealand side that had displayed plenty of batting in narrowly failing to score 479 to win the first Test. Here at Lord's, they replied to England's effort with a massive 551 for 9 declared (Congdon, Burgess and Pollard all scoring centuries, and Hastings not far short with 86). England therefore needed nearly three hundred to make New Zealand bat again.

The second time around they made a better showing, thanks to 92 from Geoff Boycott and a 'brilliantly defiant' 178 from Keith Fletcher. Only four wickets were down as they avoided the innings defeat but then, one by one, the wheels began to come off as the Kiwi spinners took the reins. First to go was Illingworth (22), after a stand of 61 with Fletcher; then, in quick succession, Alan Knott (0), Chris Old (7) and John Snow (0). With two hours still to play, England were just 70 ahead. New Zealand needed only to dispose of numbers 10 and 11 for a comfortable canter to victory – the first time they would ever have beaten England in 44 attempts.

Arnold got the thinnest of edges to his first ball from off-spinner Vic Pollard and wicket-keeper Ken Wadsworth spilled it. Two balls later, Arnold edged a firmer catch into Wadsworth's gloves – and it came straight out again. Arnold (23 not out) then played out time with Fletcher in a stand of 92, and New Zealand's chance had gone. It was to be another four years before, finally, they registered that first-ever win over England. There is a bittersweet side to the story – the likeable Ken Wadsworth didn't live to see that victory. He died three years later at the age of only 29.

Durham Pull the Petals Off the White Rose

Yorkshire v Durham, 1st round Gillette Cup, Harrogate, June 1973

'No minor county will ever beat a first-class county,' Gordon Ross wrote in the Cricketer when the Gillette Cup was introduced. This might have been a rash prediction, but nobody expected this particular tie to provide the upset. Yorkshire, after all, had won the Cup in 1965 and 1969, and had been county champions seven times in the twelve years preceding 1969. They were still reckoned the hardest side to beat. Yorkshire won the toss, Boycott elected to bat and, for a few overs at least, the world continued to spin on its axis. And then, with the score on 18, Durham's opening bowler, John Wilkinson, bowled Boycott.

There should be a pause while that sinks in. John Wilkinson bowled Boycott.

'The effect upon the Durham side was amazing,' wrote David Lemmon some years later. 'Suddenly they were like a team possessed. Their bowling was forked with fire; their fielding touched unsuspected heights.' Yorkshire's batsmen, containing four England caps, simply disintegrated in the face of ruthless pressure as they stumbled to 49 for five. Apart from Colin Johnson (44), there seemed no determination to collect themselves and fight back. Five were clean bowled, one caught behind as the Yorkshire innings closed for 135 in 58.4 overs. All the Durham bowlers returned excellent figures, but their captain, Brian Lander, was outstanding, with five for 15 in 11.4 overs.

Had Durham's nerve failed in their pursuit of the small victory total, this chapter would not exist. They won, of course, by five wickets, taking 51 overs to overhaul Yorkshire, a triumph that astounded and delighted almost everybody. Two famous sporting brothers were playing against each other that day, and the difference in their performances, slight as it was, symbolised the manner in which Durham achieved victory. The England opening bowler, Chris Old, sent down eight overs for Yorkshire and conceded fifteen runs. Miserly stuff, but his brother Alan, the England rugby international, illustrated the even tighter pressure applied by Durham, allowing a mere ten runs off his seven overs. The mighty had approached the match over-confident and unprepared, and they choked on the pressure. 'I offer humble, but the warmest possible, congratulations to Durham,' wrote Gordon Ross.

Ashes to Ashes, Dust to Dust

Australia v England, 4th Test, Sydney, January 1975

Twenty years after Typhoon Tyson had wrecked Australia with sheer speed, Dennis Lillee and Jeff Thomson exacted revenge on the Poms. Rigby's famous cartoon captured the mood perfectly. In it, five beaming undertakers wade through a sea of beer cans bearing a coffin containing a bandaged and battered English lion. In the background, Lillee and Thomson, still hurling cricket balls like hand grenades, are restrained by a sixth undertaker with the words 'Down, boys, down! It's all over.'

'Coming fresh to this series is like walking into a pitched battle between the Mafia and the IRA. You couldn't believe it was this uncompromising, this violent or this uncouth,' reported Ian Wooldridge for the *Daily Mail*. 'Practically none of the traditional courtesies of cricket survived the second day of this fourth Test.' It was alleged by John Woodcock that one of the tourists began a letter home: 'I got a half-volley the other day – in the nets.'

This all created the impression that England had capitulated spinelessly in the face of 'Lillian Thomson' and Max Walker, the third Australian quick. Such an impression does little justice to England's fortitude in these days before helmets had been introduced. On the other hand, while they were unquestionably outclassed, coming into the fifth day with all their wickets intact they should, with resolution, have saved the match once they weathered the initial onslaught and got to 68 without loss. Greig got a feisty 54 but, unforgivably, was stumped off spinner Ashley Mallett. It was left to John Edrich to show what could have been. He had two ribs broken by the first ball he received, but returned to the crease to battle to the end for 33 not out. The three Aussie pacemen took 14 wickets between them as England, having surrendered a 110-run deficit on first innings, were bundled out for 228 the second time around, to lose by 171 runs and go three for nought down in the six-match series. In the final Test, England showed what might have been, but for the raw pace and hostility of 'Lillian Thomson' (Lillee and Thomson). The back half of the lady was ruled out by injury, and the front half broke down after delivering just six balls. England went on to win by an innings.

The jokers in the pack were the Sydney crowds. Pom-bashing is mighty thirsty work, and a record presence of 178,027 consumed 864,000 cans of beer. That's nearly five per person. No wonder Rigby's cartoon showed a flying beer can clanging off the embattled lion's head!

Oh Dear, What Can the Matter Be...

England v Australia, 2nd Test, Lord's, July–August 1975

If you're under about forty, you probably can't recall the deep depression suffered by England supporters after their team's mauling by 'Lillian Thomson' – Dennis Lillee and Jeff Thomson' – in Australia in the winter of 1974–5. Within weeks, the Aussies had followed their prey to their native shores, first for the inaugural World Cup of 1975, and then to carry on the relentless mauling of the hapless Englishmen in a four-Test series. The first Test went much as matters had gone down under. Lillee took seven wickets, and Thomson five, as England crashed to defeat by an innings and 85 runs.

Naturally, the selectors made changes for the second Test, the most surprising being that of giving the critical No 3 position to a prematurely greying 33-year-old, blinking out through steel-rimmed glasses as he impersonated a lecturer in sociology from one of the newer universities. His name was David Steele, and outside Northamptonshire few had heard of him. Was this really the man to blunt Australia's terrible fast-bowling twins? With a nervous giggle, we all sat back and awaited the worst, which was not long in coming. England made a sickeningly familiar start: 10 for one. In the dressing room, 'Old Grandad', as Thommo was soon to christen him, picked up his bat and trudged downstairs for his appointment with destiny but failed, for what seemed an eternity, to emerge on the pavilion steps. Indeed, he must have been perilously close to making history by being given out for taking too long to come to the wicket. What had happened? In a nutshell, Steele went to the loo, but not for reasons of nature. For county games, he was accustomed to the visitors' dressing room but, as an England player, found himself lodged in the unfamiliar quarters of the home side. He had headed off downstairs all right and, seeing no familiar exit, had carried on – down and down – until he emerged in the basement toilets. This didn't seem right. Where was the straining Lillee, and why could he not hear the trumpeting Thommo?

After such a constipated beginning, disaster must surely follow? It did, but not at Steele's end. While England slumped to 49 for four, Steele got on to the front foot and held fast until someone with equal resolve joined the fight. With new skipper Tony Greig, he put on 96 and broke the psychological chains in which Australia had imprisoned the home side. Steele got 50, and returned to the pavilion (which he re-entered by the orthodox route) a national hero. He went on to average 60.8 in his six Test innings that summer, and was voted BBC Sportsman of the Year. 'I don't like bowling at Old Grandad,' commented Jeff Thomson. 'He's hard to get out and everybody's on his side.' England were not beaten again that year, although they failed to recover the Ashes, but history fails to record if their superstitious batsmen insisted on a lucky loo-call before going to the wicket.

Steele's beginning was a triumph, but that series also saw a disastrous debut. A promising young Essex batsman followed the same path as poor Fred Grace 95 years earlier and bagged a pair in his first Test. He froze in the face of Australia's fearsome attack, and although given a second chance at Lord's only managed 6 and 31. Luck was certainly against him. It took a good player even to touch the ball that got him first time, and his second innings delivery was unplayable. But clearly, the lad didn't have a big-match temperament, did he? He'd have to go. It wasn't for long. Graham Gooch became England's heaviest scorer, and the only man to record a triple-hundred and a century in the same Test match.

As a footnote, David Steele played throughout the notorious 1976 series against the West Indies. In his eight-Test career he scored one century and five fifties and, without any not-outs to help, averaged 48.07 – bettered among Englishmen only by Sutcliffe, Barrington, Hammond, Hobbs, Hutton and Compton. His reward was to be dropped for the winter tour of India. The selectors choked at the prospect of sending him, just in case he wasn't so good against the spinners! As consolation, Steele had 308 lamb chops stashed in the freezer to see him through the winter. An enterprising local butcher had promised him one for every run he scored against the Windies.

When the Losers Had the Last Laugh

West Indies v India, 3rd & 4th Tests, Port of Spain & Kingston, 1976

'They resembled Napoleon's troops on the retreat from Moscow,' said Dicky Rutnagur of the Indian team as they tottered towards their homeward plane following the fourth and final Test of their series against the West Indies. Some of them could barely be distinguished through cocoons of plaster and bandages, and to say they were glad to be on their way was probably an understatement. Yet only a fortnight earlier, they had been a very much happier bunch.

India went down heavily in the first Test, jet-lagged after a long flight from New Zealand and insufficient acclimatisation, but had fully recovered for the second, which they drew and, but for dropped catches, might easily have won. For the Test in Port of Spain, Trinidad, traditionally a turner in those days, the Windies selectors decided that the thing captain Clive Lloyd most ardently desired was as many spinners in the team as possible. Clive wasn't at all sure he agreed, but was given little choice in the matter. Remember, the Windies hadn't yet come to the boiling point of their invincible years. At this moment, the temperature was merely rising, and it was these next two Tests that were to prove decisive in

113

dictating the future composition of their world-beating team.

Poor Imtiaz Ali didn't know this, of course, as he received the happy news of his first West Indian cap, and probably fell asleep dreaming of a long and distinguished career, not to mention a spot of fame and a lot of fortune. Alas for ambition. He was destined never to play for his country again. Nevertheless, it all started promisingly enough. After the Windies had made 359, Imtiaz claimed two of the three wickets their spinners took as India subsided to an unthreatening 228, which enabled Clive Lloyd to declare his second innings at 271 for six. No doubt he took due note of the fact that Bedi, Chandra and Venkat, India's three great spin bowlers, were turning the ball nicely on the wearing wicket, and had achieved between them all six wickets to fall.

Presented with such a lip-smacking track on which to display their skills, the West Indian spinners, Jumadeen, Padmore and Imtiaz, must have emerged from the pavilion with a spring in their heels. It didn't last. India happily set about scoring 406 to win the match and lost only four wickets in the process. It was the highest successful last innings run chase in Test history, and only the second to pass 400. The spinners conceded 220 of those runs. It was no surprise that Clive Lloyd looked somewhat stern as he left the field. 'Gentlemen,' he asked in the dressing room, 'how many runs do you need to bowl a team out?'

After some equally well-chosen words to the selectors, his side for the final Test looked very different. From now on, pace was to be his weapon of attack, and attack was exactly what he meant – Holding ('Whispering Death') and Daniel to open the bowling, with Julien and Holder as first change. Batting first, India fought their way to 306 for six. The pitch was alarming, with variable bounce at both ends, and the cricket was, as Wisden discreetly put it, 'combative'. Two of India's batsmen had already retired hurt, and Vishwanath had broken a finger. Skipper Bedi complained to the umpires – only to be informed by Ralph Gosein that a ridge had suddenly appeared in the pitch! Moles with overactive thyroids, no doubt. Bedi therefore declared to ensure that at least his bowlers remained intact for the challenge ahead.

Indeed, despite not batting through, India conceded a lead of only 85 on first innings but, with three of his top six batsmen unable to take any further part, it was enough. India's fifth second-innings wicket fell with the score on 97. The West Indians waited patiently for the next batsman; the umpires became restive, and sent to enquire what might be happening. Nothing stirred. India's innings had ground to a halt, there being no further fit men to put on armour and venture into battle. West Indies could see their way ahead, and the cricketing world was to be shown it the hard way – though whether cricket as a whole gained remains debatable.

Batting Order?
We'll Open With Extras

England v West Indies, 3rd Test,
Old Trafford, July 1976

With their new-found policy of relentless speed (recognised spinners bowled just 31 overs in the five-Test series), West Indies came to England in 1976 with a score or two to settle with the home captain, Tony Greig. They had not forgotten his notorious run-out of Alvin Kallicharan off the last ball of the day's play in the first Test at Port of Spain in February 1974, as the players were turning towards the pavilion to put their feet up. And then, in what must go down as one of the most misplaced jokes in cricketing history, Greig had publicly declared in the off-season that the West Indies would grovel when they came up against England in their own back yard. They have a fine sense of fun in the Caribbean, but not quite along these lines. Who's a silly-billy, then?

Nevertheless, the first two Tests were drawn, and each side could feel it had been on top in one of them. Then came Old Trafford. On the first day West Indies recovered from 26 for four (which would have been 26 for five had Greenidge not been dropped) to make 211, of which Greenidge made 134. From then on, England were overwhelmed on a pitch of irregular bounce. In their first innings, the only batsman to reach double figures was David Steele with 20, and his effort was closely followed by a gritty effort from Extras who, by dint of eight byes and eleven no-balls, contributed 19 to England's pathetic 71 all out. At this date, no side apart from Australia had ever dismissed England for so few, and just to prove that irregular bounce did not make for unplayable conditions, the Windies notched up 411 for five declared in their second innings. Greenidge added 101 to his first-innings century to become only the second West Indian to make centuries in each innings of a Test.

So England found themselves going in a second time, a small matter of 551 runs adrift and eighty minutes of the third day remaining. Those eighty minutes were soon to be labelled 'infamous'. John Woodcock reported that 'the West Indian fast bowling was more hostile by far than at Trent Bridge or Lord's. Holding and Daniel, and to a lesser extent Roberts, bowled far too short.' Brian Close (aged 45) and John Edrich (39), with the highest combined age for a Test opening pair since Gunn and Sandham 46 years earlier, heroically withstood a high-speed assault, much of it aimed directly at their bodies. In those 80 minutes, the pair managed 21 runs, and it took Close 77 minutes to add to his opening single. At one point, he was hit just below the throat, and momentarily seemed to stagger. But 'The Old Blighter', as his Somerset team affectionately called him, was not a man to give ground to anyone, and the pair stood firm until stumps.

Next morning the Sunday papers were virtually unanimous in their outrage at the West Indian tactics. Australian David Frith wrote that he had 'seen the game at its most abhorrently cynical. The cricket came close to blood sport.' There was even muttering about Bodyline being reintroduced. Whether as a result of the wholesale condemnation, or whether they felt they had repaid the 'grovelling' jibe with interest, the Windies fast bowlers kept the ball well up on the fourth day, and were quickly rewarded with the merry tinkle of falling wickets. The opening stand reached 54, but was the only really effective resistance, as England's innings closed for 126, and they went down to a massive defeat by 425 runs.

The 24 made by Edrich proved to be England's highest individual score of the match – the highest, that is, except for good old Extras who, with an impressive 25, again showed no inclination to grovel. This was only the fourth time in Test history that Extras had top-scored in an innings. More remarkable still, the aggregate of Extras in England's two innings combined came to 44, surpassing the match aggregates of Steele (35), Edrich (32) or any other player. Tony Greig uttered no more jokes until he met Kerry Packer later that year.

'Methought I Heard a Voice Cry "Sleep No More"'

New Zealand v Australia, 1st Test, Christchurch, February 1977

The pitch was green when Glenn Turner won the toss and sent Australia in to bat, and when Doug Walters strolled in with the score at 112 for four the decision looked justified. At 208 for six, Gary Gilmour joined Walters and by the close they had put on 137 for the seventh wicket – 129 to Walters, 65 to Gilmour. Next man in Kerry O'Keeffe reckoned he'd better have a quiet night. If he played a big innings it might be the difference between a match-winning total, and a score which would lead to nothing better than a draw. Like all the Aussies you've ever known and loved, he had the lights out by 11.00 p.m. and went straight to sleep.

It may have been around two in the morning, but was probably even later, when persistent hammering on his door roused him from childlike slumber. Carefully putting on the chain, he inched the door open to see the cheery faces of Walters and Gilmour begging – no, insisting – that he join them for a few nightcaps. Convinced by the evidence before his eyes that he'd be batting by one minute past eleven next day, he explained, in the uncomplicated terms any Australian would understand, that as he was the poor sod who was obviously going to be in the firing line first thing he, at least, was going to get some good kip. Walters and Gilmour did not, reputedly, receive this patriotic news with the enthusiasm one might have expected and went in search of further nightcaps unaccompanied.

On the coach to the ground next morning, the two not-out batsmen grabbed some shuteye, thus missing the skipper's tactical talk for the day. They put in a few more horizontal moments while their team-mates limbered up on the pitch before play started. O'Keeffe was padded up ready as they stumbled out to the wicket, Gilmour dropping his bat on the way. Kerry was a hyperactive lad thereafter, leaping to his feet and picking up his gloves every time they played and missed. Any minute now, he'd be out there taking guard.

After thirty minutes or so of this, Doug Walters reached his 150. A little while more, and the public address system crackled into life to announce a new record Australian seventh-wicket partnership, breaking that held by Rod Marsh and a certain Kerry O'Keeffe. The next milestone was the 200 partnership, of which the second hundred had been rattled up in just 71 minutes. Finally, Gary Gilmour arrived at his maiden Test century. At this point he lost his presence of mind and was out for 101, ending a partnership of 217. The time for O'Keeffe's great innings had arrived.

No, he wasn't out first ball – though he was dropped behind on nought. The great stand, for which he'd prepared so carefully, had staggered along to 29, when he enthusiastically called his sleeping partner for a quick leg-bye and was run out for eight. Walters – whose impish sense of humour may or may not have contrived a 'wait, yes, no' situation – managed to keep a straightish face as O'Keeffe trudged up the pitch on his way to the pavilion, but as he drew alongside a loud guffaw broke the reproachful silence.

Australia finally closed on 552, of which Doug Walters got exactly 250, but they hadn't made enough to put New Zealand away by an innings. In reply, the Kiwis scored 357, saving the follow-on by just five runs. O'Keeffe, with plenty of sleep to keep him going, wheeled away to take five for 101. With tighter bowling in Australia's second knock, and some stubborn batting in their own second attempt, New Zealand held out for a draw with two wickets still intact, the obdurate Bev Congdon making a not-out century in four and a half hours. Kerry O'Keeffe's match analysis was right after all. It's just a pity he was so full of sleep he couldn't get the adrenaline flowing for the big innings he'd promised himself!

'Hey, Mate, You've Left a Stump Standing!'

Australia v Pakistan, 1st Test, Melbourne, March 1979

An average daily crowd of 7,500 in a ground holding 100,000 meant a lot of people missed an entertaining match. The pitch had early life, but nothing to excuse two low-scoring first knocks, brightened only by fast bowler Rod Hogg's dismissal. Rod strolled out of his crease before the ball was dead, an alert Pakistani whipped off the bails and umpire Clarence Harvey (brother of Neil, the great Aussie left-hander) raised the finger. The Pakistanis, mindful that they'd shortly be facing Rod with ball in hand, suggested the decision be revoked. It wasn't, and the aggrieved Rod exacted horrible vengeance on the stumps as he departed. 'I was surprised,' commented Graham Yallop, the Australian captain. 'He left one stump standing.'

Pakistan batted with aggression and flair the second time around, especially Majid Khan (108) and Zaheer Abbas (59). Their second-wicket stand of 135, full of brilliant strokeplay, was easily the biggest so far, and when Pakistan eventually declared at 353 for nine, Australia faced a mammoth 382 to win.

At 117 for two overnight, the Aussies lost Yallop to a stupid run-out on the last morning, but by four-thirty one of the great fourth innings wins was within reach, thanks to a record stand

122

of 177 between Alan Border (105) and Kim Hughes (84). With concentration and controlled aggression they saw off the second new ball and were nearing victory when all hell broke loose in the shape of that 'loveable rogue' Sarfraz Nawaz. A beautiful off-cutter bowled Border, and the remaining Aussies went as rigid as fish fingers in a freezer. Sarfraz grilled the lot in just 33 deliveries and 305 for three became 310 all out in barely ten overs. Not even 1990s England could have matched that, and a game that was on Australia's plate an hour earlier was lost by 71 runs. Sarfraz finished with nine for 86 in what Wisden called 'one of the greatest bowling feats in the history of Test cricket'.

A Mad Interlude in a Serious Drama

England v Australia, 3rd Test, Headingley, July 1981

Any England supporter old enough to remember Headingley 1981 must surely regard it as the most thrillingly heroic Test upset of their lifetime. Ian Botham's antics with the bat and Bob Willis's determination with the ball had become the stuff of legends before the summer was out. Twenty years on, the retelling of those events has the same power to irritate Australians as praising the discernment of Russian linesmen has to annoy Germans – and thereby gives Englishmen enormous pleasure! But spare a thought for the Aussies. They had the game comfortably won, even after Botham's extraordinary ton. 56 for one, needing 130 to win, and they blew it. When the game was stolen from them, they were shattered. From that moment they were psychologically beaten, and a series they had led 1–0 was lost 3–1.

The story of the first three and a half days is quickly told. Batting first, Australia declared at 401 for nine, and then, on the third day, Lillee, Alderman and Lawson stretched England's batting on the rack of a pitch already cutting and seaming. Even so, 174 was a dismal score, made worse when, following on, Gooch went without scoring just before the close of play. At

227 behind with only nine wickets intact, the England team prepared themselves for the gloom of an innings defeat and, along with most of their supporters, they understandably cancelled their hotel bookings for the fourth night of the game. Slightly more surprisingly, perhaps, one or two Australian players took odds of 500–1 on England to win, and blew a tenner apiece. But then cricket's a funny old game, isn't it, and what's a tenner when, in your heart of hearts, you know you've got the game sewn up?

There was probably nobody in the crowd on the fourth and fifth days who was asking himself what constitutes a funny old game, much less expecting a practical demonstration, but that was exactly what he was privileged to witness. Boycott was Boycott for three and a half hours and 46 runs, but when Graham Dilley joined Botham at the crease the score was 135 for seven and England were still 92 runs away from avoiding an innings defeat.

'The match was lost,' said Botham, 'so we decided to have a go. Dilley and I laughed and joked, seeing who could play the most idiotic stroke. For two hours we swiped and the score rattled up on the board. It was a gambler's last throw.' The ball was cutting, shooting and lifting. In such conditions, the Aussies had to keep plenty of close fielders near the bat but, as both batsmen admitted, if you attack, anything can happen. You can miss the ball by a foot, carve it over the slips or hit it for six, and all of these things happened. The Australians lost control. 'I had no idea we were already in front when Dilley (56) was out,' said Botham afterwards. 'I thought we were still behind.' But in front they were, by 25 runs, and with Chris Old scoring an invaluable 29, England were all out early on the fifth morning for 356, a lead of 129. Botham was not out 149, and with literal truth Wisden described his innings as unforgettable.

Nevertheless, Australia should have had little problem wrapping up the game on the last day, and taking an unassailable

2–0 lead in the series, especially when they were a mere 74 runs from victory with nine wickets in hand. In hindsight, this ignores three factors – the mental fragility caused by England's second-innings batting assault, Bob Willis, and the psychological manipulation of skipper Mike Brearley. Brearley made Willis open the bowling into the wind, to get his adrenalin, and his temper, flowing. When Willis changed ends to bowl with the wind behind him, he was like a man inspired. 'It is not uncommon to see him perform for England as if his very life depended on it,' reported Wisden, 'but this was something unique.' Watch a video recording of Willis bowling that day, and look at his face. You see a man whose concentration is so complete that nothing else exists. The Australians simply crumpled before this combination of naked willpower and outstanding bowling. Those nine wickets tumbled for 55 runs, and England had 'stretched the bounds of logic and belief' to win by 18 runs.

It's a Funny Old Game...

Essex v Surrey,
Chelmsford, May 1983

You've got a better chance of winning the lottery than of never having heard someone, somewhere, say, 'It's a funny old game, cricket.' Being the May bank holiday, there would have been more than the usual few stragglers around the boundary's edge for the second day of the Essex–Surrey game in 1983. Essex made up for time lost the previous Saturday and, untroubled, carried their first-innings score to 287, with Fletcher completing a polished 110. Everything seemed routinely predictable, even if the humid atmosphere suggested ideal conditions for swinging the ball. It would have occurred to nobody that they were about to witness cricket so funny that they would want to rush home, impatient to beget children who would beget grandchildren to whom they could relate the amazing tale.

Had you loitered in the beer tent that afternoon as Surrey began their reply, you might have emerged to glance at the scoreboard, rubbed your eyes and concluded you must have had more pints than Surrey had runs. The scoreboard read eight for eight, and Sylvester Clarke was on his way out to join Monkhouse. The last six batsmen had all made ducks. This kind of thing didn't happen in modern times. All those record low scores – 12, 13, 15 – surely belonged to cricket's Jurassic period a century or so ago? Monkhouse probably thought cricket was far too funny for him as he edged the ball to the slips – and through them, for two. Double figures! Respectability! At the other end, Clarke ruined Neil Foster's figures (four for 10) by swinging lustily to mid-wicket for the only boundary, before Foster yorked him and Norbert Phillip (six for four) accounted for Monkhouse. Fourteen was luxury. Back in pre-history, after all, four sides had been dismissed for less.

Next day, Surrey were soon 18 for two as they followed on and then, with as little warning as the earlier shenanigans had started, normality returned. Clinton (61) and Knight (101) batted comfortably to the close, and the game subsided to a gentle draw. It's a funny old game...

Classic, Palm-sweating Tension

India v West Indies, World Cup Final, Lord's, June 1983

You don't need to be thinning on top to remember how the West Indies bestrode the cricketing world like a colossus in the twenty years before the mid 1990s. That domination probably began with their seizure of the first World Cup in 1975, and by 1979 their retention of it was no surprise. Were they overconfident when they took the field against India in the 1983 final, ready to make it a hat-trick? Not that they should have underestimated their opponents who, in the space of six days, had disposed of Australia and England en route to Lord's which, on Final day, Wisden declared was 'groomed like a high-born lady'.

Srikkanth set about the Windies attack with a medley of what Chris Martin-Jenkins called 'glorious hooks, cuts, drives and ghastly village-green heaves'. When he fell for 38, making it 59 for two, nobody in the capacity crowd could have believed it would be the highest score of the game. Either side of lunch, India lost four wickets in a careless blaze of extravagance, and when their innings closed for 183 the game had gone much as everyone expected. Observing the Indian medium-pacers getting more out of the conditions than the

129

West Indians, umpire Dickie Bird reckoned 240 would have given them a chance.

The Indian captain, Kapil Dev, didn't agree. When Haynes fell, to make it 50 for two, he wandered the field muttering, 'We've got them now. They think it's too easy.' If Viv Richards seemed to mock this prediction with seven searing boundaries, his mistimed pull, followed immediately by Clive Lloyd's untimely pull of his groin muscle, somersaulted the match from foregone conclusion to nail-biting apprehension. West Indies needed to gamble, to deploy their attacking genius, but caution and accumulation overcame attack as the tension – and the Indian bowling – grew ever tighter. Only one boundary was scored in the last 17 overs as the Windies were slowly strangled to death 43 runs short, and Indians around the world took flight in joyous celebrations.

'Prep School Stuff!'

Essex v Middlesex, Benson & Hedges Cup Final, Lord's, July 1983

Now and again, one-day finals produce finishes which cut across the expected grain, and the 1983 B&H Final was one of these. The start was delayed by nearly an hour, and the conditions were steamy, so Middlesex can't have been too thrilled at having to bat first. It showed, too, and their innings was a struggle throughout, saved only by a characteristically inventive and resolute 89 not out from Clive Radley, which enabled them to finish on a below-par 196. The young Neil Foster took three good wickets for only 26.

Essex, and Graham Gooch in particular, began their run chase like a house on fire. Gooch was imperious, taking 16 off Norman Cowan's first over, and dominating the bowling until, with the score on 79, he was caught behind for 46. In retrospect, it was the turning point of the match. What a pity for them that the Middlesex supporters who went home at tea, when the score was 113 for one and Essex needed but 84 off 30 more overs, didn't know it. 'How can we play so badly?' asked one. 'We're being made to look second class.'

At 151 for four, there still seemed little to worry Essex until, as the *Cricketer* reported, 'panic set in. With the shades of night descending, Essex went into full retreat. You name it, it happened. It was prep school stuff!' Even so, only twelve were needed off the last four overs, and still there were four wickets left. But two super catches and the traditional run-out meant five were needed off the last over with one wicket to fall. And fall it did, first ball! I met a taxi driver as I left the ground, an Essex supporter who'd been watching on television till it was time to go on duty. 'How many wickets did we win by?' he asked – and asked again. He didn't believe me the second time either.

The World's Least Accomplished No 11?

Courtney Walsh's other great record, 1984–2001

One can hardly call a number-eleven batsman an embarrassment. The whole point of being last man is to ensure maximum kipping time with your feet up, secure in the knowledge that you'll soon be out there bowling your side back into contention after the batters have screwed things up – again. But holding the world record for the number of Test-match ducks might just bring a mild flush to the cheeks.

Say the name Courtney Walsh in almost any part of the world where cricket is played, and you'll be answered with a smile. It might be a smile of admiration for an opening bowler who holds the world record number of Test wickets, and is so far the only one to capture 500; it might be a smile of affection for a loveable and sporting personality to whom almost everybody seems to warm; or it might be a smile and a giggle at the thought of Courtney's batting. The awful truth is that in his otherwise distinguished career, he managed 43 – yes, forty-three – Test dismissals without scoring. Add the innumerable times he's trudged all the way out to bat, only to return on nought not out after facing the smallest number of deliveries his batting partner can contrive, and you realise that a significant portion of Courtney's life has been devoted to a spectacularly fruitless quest.

Despite it all, on the occasions he's managed to hang about his unique style has given huge enjoyment to many people. And at least one of his nought not-outs was a heroic one. In the Test against Australia at Bridgetown in 1999, he joined Brian Lara with six still needed and the Aussies rampant. He faced up to them, he survived, and the Windies achieved a superlative victory against the odds.

Border Frays Round the Edges

Australia v England, 1st Test, Brisbane, November 1986

An Ashes series down under is always a tough proposition, and when Mike Gatting's England team arrived at the Gabba for the first Test, few gave them a chance of holding on to the wee urn. Their three first-class warm-up games had not gone well: they had just been thoroughly outplayed by Western Australia. The batting had looked frighteningly insecure against the pace bowling of Bruce Reid and Chris Matthews, both of whom were promptly selected for the Test squad. David Gower had bagged a pair and his form seemed particularly fragile.

For some years, the Gabba had enjoyed a reputation as seamer-friendly, so the Aussie squad included Geoff Lawson and Merv Hughes as well as Reid and Matthews. Come the day of the match, Lawson, with 34 caps already behind him, was omitted for fear he hadn't fully recovered from back trouble. Mistake number one. By contrast, England's fast-bowling resources looked thin, with only Graham Dilley claiming genuine speed, and their slip-catching against Western Australia had been woeful. When Alan Border won the toss, one would have expected him to bat against a team close to being disheartened and with only a moderate seam attack. So what did he do? Put England in. Mistake number two. His three remaining quicks were inexperienced, with nine caps between them, and on the day it showed.

Gower came in with the score 198 for three, and a fourth wicket went down at the same score. Before he was off the mark Gower was dropped by Chris Matthews at third slip off Hughes. Mistake number three, which Phil Edmonds reckoned was 'the turning point of the whole tour'. Wisden agreed: 'It may well have decided the destination of the Ashes.' Gower (51) went on to share a stand of 118 with Ian Botham (138). England proceeded to a comfortable seven-wicket win, gained the psychological high ground and, when they won the fourth Test to go 2–0 up, were assured of returning home successful.

When Lamb Got the Bird

Not to be read by umpires of a nervous disposition, 1983 & 1987

No-one admiring Allan Lamb's heroic battles with the West Indies pace attack in the 1980s, including his centuries in three successive Tests in 1984, would have thought they were watching the game's biggest practical joker. Nor would the many admirers of umpire Dickie Bird's perceptive and authoritative control have expected him to fall victim time and again to the plots hatched against him by a straight-faced Lamb. From the safety of retirement, Dickie has gleefully retold them on many occasions. Even so, some of them bear repetition, such as the time during the fourth England–New Zealand Test at Trent Bridge in 1983 when Lamb waited for Dickie to settle into his familiar hunch over the wicket at the bowler's end before letting off a string of firecrackers behind him.

On another occasion, Lambie brightened a dullish county game by setting fire to the umpire's room after quietly locking a trustingly unaware Dickie inside. Once his nerves had settled, the Great Adjudicator dropped his biggest clanger by dispensing forgiveness for this naughty prank instead of exacting dire revenge, and at the end of the game went to the car park with a comforting sense of relief at the prospect of being out of Mr Lamb's clutches for a while. He found his car up on bricks, with neither the four wheels nor the aforesaid Mr Lamb anywhere to be seen.

A less well-known jolly jape took place during the 1987 World Cup on the subcontinent. Dickie dropped another clanger by contracting fever, and spent three days in bed feeling extremely sorry for himself. At first, all went well. The English team were generous with their visits and get-well gifts to the suffering victim – until Allan Lamb decided it was time for a more unorthodox method of stimulating the patient. Flinging open the door of Dickie's room, he marched in a group of well-armed security guards and lined them up with the order, 'Right. Put the poor bugger out of his misery. Ready! Take aim! Fire!' Of course, you know the one about the mobile phone, the umpire and Messrs Lamb and Botham? Yes you do. Everyone does.

It Took a Minefield to Bring the Series Alive

India v Pakistan, 5th Test, Bangalore, March 1987

International contests in any sport should be occasions when, whatever the result, our admiration is reserved for the skill of the participants and, irrespective of media bleating, the result is of secondary importance. But, more often than not, when India and Pakistan play each other politics seem to induce more palpitations than an umpire reaching for his light meter. Avoiding defeat has, on too many occasions, appeared to be the only thing on the players' minds. Indeed, relations between the two countries have sometimes become so fraught that cricket has not been played at all – between 1955 and 1978, for example, only one series was staged, and there have been only 47 Tests between the two in half a century.

The India–Pakistan rubber of 1987 followed a run of seven successive draws, and when the first four Tests of this series, played on shirt-front wickets, of which Ramaswamy Mohan wrote that they 'blunted the edge of Pakistan's pace attack and provided nothing for spin bowlers', also finished in languorous draws, it appeared that the age of seemingly permanent stalemate had returned to the subcontinent. This impression was hardly allayed by the bizarre events of the fourth Test.

After the second day's play, a violent thunderstorm broke over the Jaipur ground, sweeping away the polythene sheet protecting the docile wicket. The following morning, there was found to be sawdust on the pitch. Pakistan complained that the wicket had been tampered with and its nature altered, India protested that the storm had blown the sawdust onto the pitch, and the umpires solved the stand-off by declaring the day did not exist, thus shortening the match by 20 per cent.

The decisive fifth Test was scheduled for Bangalore, a pitch notorious for its flatness. What the captains found was (Mohan again) '660 square feet of unprepared turf, a minefield which did more for result-orientated cricket than all the protestations.' It has been suggested that India's cricket administrators were increasingly dismayed by the dull, featureless cricket the series had produced, and encouraged the preparation of a wicket likely to produce a result. If true, they deserve great credit, even if the outcome was not precisely the one they would have wished.

Pakistan elected to bat first, and almost at once were shocked to find the ball turning square. Seeming to decide that survival was impossible, they chose to play extravagant shots, presumably reckoning they might as well garner what runs they could, while they could. It was a policy born of panic, and they were tumbled out in 49 overs for 116. So small a first-innings score has hardly ever won a Test match. All India needed to do was observe what had undone Pakistan and play with common sense, defending with care and accumulating runs carefully. Time was not an issue. Indeed, as they passed 100 with only three wickets down, a significant lead beckoned, but when Dilip Vengsarkar (50) gave Tauseef Ahmed his fourth consecutive wicket with the score on 102, the Indian innings fell to pieces. Failing to learn from Pakistan's first-innings suicide, the Indians also perished through headlong aggression, and were all out for 145, a lead of only 29.

Pakistan were back in the game, and this time they applied the lessons which India had spurned. They 'clung to the crease' to build an unspectacular but challenging 249, helped by the failure of the Indian spinners to understand that, however helpful the pitch, you still have to bowl with thought and effort. Where Maninder Singh had taken seven for 27 in 18 overs in the first innings, now it took him 44 overs to capture three for 99. When India went in, seeking 221 for victory, one man demonstrated how the game could and should have been won. In the previous match, Sunil Gavaskar, the Little Maestro, had become the first man to reach 10,000 Test runs. Now he gave a masterclass in how to bat on a spiteful wicket, making 96 peerless runs, far and away the game's highest score, before a doubtful slip catch saw his departure 35 short of victory. Nobody else managed more than 26, and India lost by 16 runs. You can throw away a game through failure of nerve, but lack of proper thought and application can do the job just as effectively, as Gavaskar's gem of an innings had demonstrated only too clearly to his team-mates.

Fury in Fisalabad – or Were We in Faisalabad?

Pakistan v England, 2nd Test, Faisalabad, December 1987

Like methane gas leaking imperceptibly from the ground, a cloud of mistrust had been gathering between England and Pakistan. It was finally ignited by the sparks that flew between umpire Shakoor Rana and England captain Mike Gatting with three balls left of the second day's play at Faisalabad. The fireball it created was quite a spectacle while it lasted.

Ever since the first tour to Pakistan in 1961, England's cricketers had felt that playing skills were always going to be subordinate to umpiring machinations in winning matches, while the Pakistanis' 1980 and 1987 experiences in England had engendered similar feelings in them. Nor was it the cleverest of ideas to arrange a winter series between the two countries on the heels of a five-Test series in England the previous summer, and the subsequent World Cup on the subcontinent. After such a workload, neither set of players was in the sunniest of moods.

Trouble had quickly flared in the first Test at Lahore. Play started on a used pitch, tailor-made for Abdul Qadir's leg spin (which he duly exploited with brilliance to return figures of nine for 56 and four for 45) in front of 200 spectators who, intentionally or not, had sidled through the gates. After their World Cup failure, the Pakistani team was not riding high in public interest or esteem. England had started the tour expecting the worst of the umpiring, and in this sense they were not to be disappointed, believing themselves the victims of nine bad decisions. When Chris Broad was given out in the second innings, caught behind off Iqbal Qasim, he could be prised from the wicket only after a talking-to by fellow-opener Graham Gooch. Every England official in sight leapt, unwisely, into post-match condemnation of the umpiring, thus ratcheting the tension ever tighter.

Imagine, therefore, the joy with which England received the glad tidings, as they arrived in Faisalabad for the second Test, that Shakoor Rana was to stand. This was the umpire with, it appeared, a genius for getting under the skin of foreign cricketers, to such an extent that, two years earlier, skipper Jeremy Coney had led his Kiwis off the field in protest. The fuse had been lit, and what Wisden described as 'one of the most acrimonious Test matches in history' got under way.

The flashpoint arrived with three deliveries left on the second day. England had performed above themselves in making 292, well beyond par for the pitch conditions, and Pakistan were struggling at 106 for five. Salim Malik was batting, and Gatting moved David Capel up from square leg to save a possible single. As Eddie Hemmings was about to bowl, Shakoor halted play on the grounds that Gatting was moving a player behind the batsman's back, and the pair were off. 'Within seconds,' reported Martin Johnson, 'the two were locked in a toe-to-toe, finger-wagging exchange.' According to the players within earshot, Shakoor accused Gatting of being 'a f****** cheating c***'. 'The language employed throughout was basic,' Wisden acknowledged. Play was suspended for the rest of the day, for the whole of the third day, and demands for apology flew backwards and forwards on into the succeeding rest day. At one stage, it appeared Gatting and Shakoor were prepared to exchange apologies but, it was alleged, the Pakistan captain Javed Miandad had little enthusiasm for an early restart, his team being in too much danger of losing the match, and vetoed any such idea. The England players let it be known that they would refuse to play if Gatting was ordered to make a unilateral apology. Well-fed Pakistani officials seemed always to be 'out to dinner' when anyone tried to find them to discuss a way out. It began to look as if a string of UN resolutions would be needed to make any headway.

And then the TCCB – 'in the wider interests of the game', you understand – did, indeed, demand a unilateral apology from Gatting who thus, between teeth so gritted that not even he would have been able to force down a ham sandwich, penned one of history's shorter surrender treaties: 'I apologise for the bad language used during the second day of the Test match at Fisalabad [sic].' The England players decided to play under protest and issued a statement making scathingly clear what they thought of the TCCB's view of these 'wider interests'.

When it was subsequently revealed that the TCCB had paid each player a 'hardship bonus' of £1,000 to continue, the honour of all concerned was torpedoed and sank without trace. It was a black period for cricket, and dishonoured every single person involved.

When the Big Day Out Turned to Nightmare

NatWest/Cheltenham & Gloucester Finals, Lord's, 1989, 1992 & 2001

Semi-finals are the tensest of all knockout matches. If you lose a semi, no-one remembers you a few weeks later. If you win, you've a month to enjoy the anticipation of playing at Lord's in front of a full house. Even the seasoned, high-profile players get excited by the prospect, so imagine how it feels if you're one of the junior members of the side, accustomed to playing in front of fifty spectators and five dogs. You fall asleep at night dreaming that the skipper tosses you the ball, hoping you'll keep it tight, and you whip out the batsmen who were threatening to take the match away from you. The crowd cheers as you hold up the Man of the Match award... Sweet dreams, but sometimes they go hideously wrong and turn into nightmares.

Simon Hughes was no tyro as he prepared to bowl the last over in the 1989 final against Warwickshire. Aged thirty, he was in his eighth season with Middlesex, and was the side's acknowledged last over specialist. Warwickshire needed ten to win, and on strike was the inexperienced Neil Smith whose contract, it was said, might not be renewed at the end of the season. Instead of bowling a fast straight ball, Hughes decided on a slower one. It worked – well, nearly! Smith launched his

145

whirlwind drive a fraction too early, but still he caught it a tremendous crack. 'Catch it!' yelled the bowler, as the ball rocketed into orbit. It was caught, 'by a bloke in the ninth row of the upper stand,' Hughes recalled. Just to complete the mayhem, the thunderstruck Hughes then bowled a wide and Warwickshire cantered happily home. Middlesex supporters, who reckoned they had the trophy in their hands, couldn't believe what they were seeing. 'People who'd asked for my autograph before that day were handing it back afterwards,' the shamefaced culprit admitted years later.

Justin Benson of Leicestershire must have looked forward to the 1992 final against Northants. Although Leicestershire were reckoned the underdogs, Northants had lost the last four finals they'd contested, so it didn't have to be the stuff of dreams to believe an upset was possible. Leicestershire made an uncertain start and it took a fine but slow partnership between Whitaker and Robinson to bring them back into the game. It was 179 for three when Benson, an acknowledged hitter, went in with licence to go for glory in the remaining six overs. Alas, even by his parsimonious standards, Curtly Ambrose was in mean mood. A slower ball, and Justin was on his way back to the pavilion in that uncomfortable silence a batsman dreads. Nor was fate finished with him. Thanks to Fordham's 91 and Rob Bailey's 72 not out, Northants cruised to victory by eight wickets. How different it might have been if Justin had managed to hang on to the slip catches each batsman gave, within two overs of each other, early in their big partnership. To giftwrap his unhappiness, the winning runs were hit off his bowling. He played five more games for Leicestershire the following season, and then left the first class arena.

But surely the biggest sympathy vote goes to Scott Boswell (Leicestershire again) for the nightmare he suffered on the big stage in the 2001 final against Somerset. In the semi-final against Lancashire he'd taken four for 44, and they were top scalps – Michael Atherton, Andy Flintoff, Neil Fairbrother and Graham Lloyd. This youngster's dreams of Final glory would have won many people's vote. And what happened? Taking the new ball, he bowled just two overs. A couple of wides and a couple of boundaries, and his confidence snapped. His rhythm and timing went completely, and his second over contained so many wides and no-balls that it took fourteen attempts to get through it. Banished to lonely third man to contemplate his misery, the ball followed him with sadistic irony and, in his desperate attempt to reach it, he dived over it and gouged a huge hole in the turf. He must have wished he could bury himself in it. 'Leicestershire have released Scott Boswell from his contract,' the newspapers reported a month or so later. Anyone who has ever played cricket will have nothing but heartfelt sympathy.

When a Single is Not a Good Idea

West Indies v Australia, 1st Test, Kingston, Jamaica, March 1991

Nobody ever thought facing the ferocious West Indies fast bowler Patrick Patterson was his idea of a jolly afternoon out. No quickie likes batsmen. Patterson hated them. And he was on a hat trick as Australia's No 11, Mike Whitney, who didn't reckon batting a favourite occupation at the best of times, edged towards the wicket. The Sabina Park crowd loves a good quickie, and reckoned the sight of a rabbit being slaughtered rewarded the price of admission.

After a quick gulp, Whitney prepared to meet his doom, but he had one trick, at least, up his sleeve. As Patterson gathered himself for his delivery stride, Whitney put up his hand and walked away to square leg. He reckoned that made a retaliatory bouncer a racing certainty. As long as he saw it, all he had to do now was duck. Patterson roared in again and Whitney ducked. It was a yorker, and to this day neither he nor the slip cordon know how the ball missed the wicket.

The next ball was – of course – a bouncer aimed at the point of Whitney's chin. Whitney flung up his bat in self-protection and, as he saw it lob over silly mid-on's head, set off for the other end with a 'Yesssss' that might have been heard in Trinidad.

There was a rumbling noise as he arrived at the non-striker's end. Attempting a straight face, umpire Steve Bucknor announced, 'Bad news, Mr Whitney. That's over,' and walked off to square leg with a deep bass chuckle. Now past caring, Whitney heaved at Courtney Walsh's first ball and it flew off the edge to fine leg for a single. David Boon, with a ton to his name, studiously blocked the five remaining balls. 'Just wanted another look at how you play Patrick Patterson, mate.' It wasn't a long look. Two more balls were enough to remove Whitney's middle stump.

The Wages of the Perfumed Harlot

England v South Africa, World Cup semi-final, Sydney, March 1992

It was Peter Roebuck who wrote, 'To adore one-day cricket is to choose a perfumed harlot,' and that became uncomfortably true as the 1992 World Cup was scheduled for the end of the Australian summer, when the weather down under is predictably unpredictable. It was the insistence of Kerry Packer's television channel that had demanded this timing, and the same source that played its part in the adoption of a ludicrous regulation regarding rain-affected games. 'If, due to a suspension of play, the number of overs in the innings of the side batting second has to be revised, their target score shall be the runs scored by the team batting first from the equivalent number of highest scoring overs, plus one.' Got it? No, nobody else did either. It was a largely untried system. It spoiled several games and, as John Woodcock said, 'South Africa's chances of reaching the final foundered on a rule which no-one had bothered to think through.'

In their semi-final against the Proteas, England, led by Graeme Hick (83), batted extraordinarily well in damp, humid conditions to make 252 for six in 45 overs. At halfway they seemed the likely winners but South Africa, in their first World

150

Cup, were a team of bonny fighters. Big hitting and adventurous running kept them in the hunt, and they needed 22 runs from 13 deliveries – a tall order with six wickets down, but possible – when a short shower interrupted proceedings. England's Derek Pringle takes up the story: 'Eleven minutes later out trudged the teams to continue, thinking that seven balls were left. In fact, there was only one ball left and South Africa needed 21 off it. A great game had ended in complete farce – due to all-powerful television schedules.' Brian McMillan (21 not out) patted a single and set off in disgust for the pavilion, as the crowd hooted its derision at the absurd ruling. As Wisden commented, it 'led to an uproar which echoed for weeks afterwards'.

A Big Hand, Please, For the Man Who Dropped Brian Lara

Warwickshire v Durham, Edgbaston, June 1994

How do you feel when, on a flat pitch, you drop the world's best batsman on 18, and have to stand behind him for another seven hours or so while he adds a further 483? I'm not sure if you would call Chris Scott, the Durham keeper on that fateful day when Lara became the first man ever to pass 500 in first-class cricket, a joker or a choker, but if it was left to me I'd invite him to join the after-dinner speech circuit and make a tidy living spinning tales around that spectacular innings. Why should Lara have all the glory? Without Scott's bloomer the rest of the world would never have enjoyed it.

All sorts of little oddities surrounded that epic innings. Anderson Cummins, the Durham opening bowler, had been twelfth man for the West Indies when, just seven weeks earlier, Lara made his record Test score of 375. Now, Cummins said, 'he could have been out first ball. I banged one in, and it lobbed off the end of his bat just out of my reach.' When he had ten, Cummins bowled him with a no-ball, and on 18, in the last-chance saloon, came Scott's notorious dropped catch.

Warwickshire's coach, Bob Woolmer, the former England batsman, is one of the few people to have seen both Hanif's 499 (see page 89) and Lara's 501 not out. As a schoolboy, he was on holiday with his parents who, in January 1959, were working in Karachi. His father dropped him off at the ground. 'I don't remember much about it. There was a big crowd, a matting wicket, a very rough outfield and a bloke getting run out!' Mushtaq Mohammed, Hanif's brother, had been playing in the Karachi game. On Lara's day he was in his Birmingham office when someone phoned him to tell him his brother's record was under attack. He jumped in his car, drove to Edgbaston, and got to the ground in time to see the players walking off after Warwickshire's declaration!

The Nightmare of a Good Man

England v West Indies, 6th Test, the Oval, August 1995

To win your first cap in the last Test of a series is not ideal. Unless your performance is seismic, there's always the likelihood you'll be seen as a mere stopgap, only half-considered for the winter tour, and forgotten in next season's fresh start. On the other hand, if you're 34 and have been distinguishing yourself on the county circuit for fifteen seasons, it's better to be given at least one chance of representing your country. Alan Wells' selection for the sixth Test against the West Indies in 1995 was popular and, indeed, 'belated', as Wisden confirmed. A consistent performer at No 4 for Sussex, and a likeable man, he was at the top of his form that summer, even by his own high standards.

England's series with the Windies was all square as the sides came to the Oval for the decider, but the pitch they found there 'had been anaesthetised for the occasion'. It helped neither seam nor spin, and a mere 22 wickets were to fall in five days of cricket. Only the speed with which the West Indies, and in particular Lara (179), compiled their massive first innings of 692 for eight declared put any kind of pressure on England, and even that was to be resisted with comfort.

This is getting ahead of the game, however. On a blameless first-day wicket, it was Curtly Ambrose (five for 96) who was to pose the one real threat. In Richard Hutton's words, Ambrose was 'the only one to land the ball on the seam with regularity, and his occasional bounce and persistent accuracy were a constant threat to England's batsmen.' England had reached 192 before Thorpe was caught behind off Ambrose for 74, and Alan Wells' big moment had arrived. His first ball rose steeply into his ribcage and he fended it off straight into the hands of Campbell at short square leg. In that moment, he must have known his Test career, for which he had waited so long, had started and finished on Thursday 24 August 1995.

You'll Be Wanting a Good Long Bowl

Sri Lanka v India, 1st Test, Colombo, August 1997

Fate seems to have made Nilesh Kulkarni's Test career its plaything. So far, he's appeared twice against Sri Lanka in 1997, once in Colombo, and at home in India three months later; and once against Australia in 2001.

'It was a terrible toss to win,' said Sachin Tendulkar, having prodded the 'dead-as-a-dodo' pitch and elected to have first use. Indeed, the Indian batting collapsed to a miserable 537 for eight before he declared towards the end of the second day to see if Sri Lanka could do any better. With 39 on the board, Tendulkar called up debutant Kulkarni who, with his very first ball, had Marvan Atapattu caught behind, whereupon the umpires removed the bails. Kulkarni went to bed with the impressive Test figures of one for nought in one ball, and the knowledge that he was the first Indian, and only the twelfth bowler in history, to take a wicket with his first Test delivery. He and his team-mates were to go to their rest twice more before another wicket fell.

Sanath Jayasuriya and Roshan Mahanama played themselves in carefully on days three and four in front of crowds in which, the *Cricketer* said, 'there were more crows than spectators'. By the morning of the fifth day, their stand was well past 500, Jayasuriya was on 326 and, encouraged by free admission, 32,000 people had displaced the complaining crows to watch him overtake Brian Lara's record 375. But with the stand within one run of the world record for any wicket (577), Mahanama unaccountably froze, and at 615 for two India sensed things swinging their way. In a humane society, Jayasuriya would have been given an hour or two to grieve for the loss of so long-standing a partner. As it was, two balls later he prodded a simple catch to silly point and was on his way for 340. Sri Lanka gritted their teeth and plodded on until the umpires gratefully removed the bails to end the match, by which time the Sri Lankans had amassed 952 for six. In the course of five days, 1489 runs had been scored and a mere fourteen wickets had fallen. In all probability, even the crows had tucked their heads under their wings long before the close.

Poor Kulkarni finished with one for 195 in 70 overs. His next Test, at Nagpur, was rained out, and three years later on a spinner's wicket he managed a match return of one for 137 against Australia. Still, it got his average down a bit, so it's not all bad news.

Thanks, Marvan – We'll Call You If We Need You

Atapattu's patient journey to stardom, 1990s

Marvan Atapattu took a long time getting the hang of this Test batting business. His first opportunity came in the only Test of Sri Lanka's tour of India in November, 1990, and he made two noughts. 'Thanks, Marvan. We'll get in touch,' they probably said, or something pithier. One year and nine months later, they gave him another go in the first Test against Australia in Colombo. Another duck in the first innings was unfortunate, but a stylish one in the second might have caught the eye had Sri Lanka not lost eight wickets for 37 runs to gift the match to Australia by 16 runs. 'It must be the greatest heist since the Great Train Robbery,' grinned Alan Border afterwards. So it was 'Thanks, Marvan. We'll call you', once more. And eighteen months later they did! Summoned for the Test against India in Ahmedabad, he did it again. Nought and nought.

At this point, a Test average of 0.166 might have suggested, however gently, a batsman devoid of big-match temperament. But there was clearly something about the lad, so two years later they took him down and dusted him off again. The results were:

1st Test v New Zealand, Dunedin, March 1997: 25 & 22.
1st Test v Pakistan, Colombo, April 1997: 0 & 25.
2nd Test v Pakistan, Colombo, April 1997: 14 & 4.
1st Test v West Indies, St Vincent, June 1997: 7 & 10.

This man couldn't middle a bread roll bowled by an octogenarian. But wait.

Without warning, this apparent dropper of clangers turned into one of the best openers around today. In his tenth Test, opening against India in November 1997, he scored 108, and followed it with 98. The penny dropped, the confidence surged. Atapattu has never looked back, as many Test bowlers have discovered in the last five years. He has now scored five double-centuries and four single-hundreds, and is among the most prized of scalps – when you can capture it.

Rummy Goings-on in the Ranji

The Ranji Trophy, India, 1997–8

In its 64 distinguished years, the Ranji Trophy had never encountered the kind of jokers that came out of the pack during the 1997–8 competition. The first was the most bizarre because it seemed to lack point or motive, but if you're addicted to the quirks and oddities of cricket, you'll appreciate it none the less. Wisden's section on Unusual Dismissals contains short lists of those naughty lads who've Handled the Ball, Obstructed the Field or Hit the Ball Twice, but there had never, in all its years, been a heading 'Timed Out' – until, in December 1997, Hemulal Yadav decided it was time to change things.

He was last man in for Tripura in their zonal match against Orissa. The latter had run up 521 for eight declared in their first innings and, in reply, Tripura had reached 235 when their ninth wicket went down. Instead of waiting for the innings to close, the umpires called a drinks break, which Yadav spent sitting near the boundary. Come the resumption, the umpires and players resumed their positions and waited for him to come and play with them. Did Yadav stiffen the sinews and summon up the blood? He did not, so the umpires declared him timed out. In the two seasons of his first-class career, his best score was

4 and his batting average 1.37. It was also the last match of his career. Perhaps it had all become too much bother on a hot day. Or perhaps he just wanted to appear in Wisden.

Two months later, Tamil Nadu and Delhi managed to get themselves disqualified from the Trophy, and, again, a drinks break was the flashpoint. Tamil had made 473 and, during the break, the two Delhi batsmen (wearing rubber-soled shoes) chatted to the umpires. Come the restart, the pitch was found to have been roughed up. Imagine the look of innocence on the faces of the Tamil Nadu fielders! But, short of invisible rabbits, who else could it have been? Although the pitch was repaired, Delhi refused to continue the game and so, for sabotage on one side, and insubordination on the other, both teams were disqualified.

An Unexpected Presence in the Team Photo

Leicestershire discover they have an extra member on the staff, 1999

It's one of the rituals of county cricket, gathering for the group photograph of the playing staff, all ready to send off to Wisden and the local paper. 'Right, lads, stop tooling around and get yourselves sat down for the squad photo. I want the gnarled old pros, the overseas mercenaries and the ones with EU passports in the front row next to the chairman. The rest of you boys that really believe we're going to give you a game one day, stand in the back rows and look as if you're up for it, right?' And so, in next season's Wisden, eighteen county reports are preceded by eighteen squad photos, most of which look identical. Usually, only doting relatives bother to look at them, but the Wisden for 2000 had an unexpectedly uplifting effect.

There appeared to be 31 people in the photo of Leicestershire's 1999 playing staff, and indeed 31 names were printed underneath, but further inspection confirmed that an extra member was present. There he was in the second row, directly in front of M T Brimson, framed by the shoulders of P Nixon and C Lewis sitting in the front row. No magnifying glass was needed to confirm that J Thomas had sneaked into the photo, unacknowledged in the caption. Was this a private joke or were the other players in on the performance? It was hard on them if they weren't.

Although he'd been awarded his cap in 1998, Brimson hadn't experienced much of a sensation with either his batting or bowling, averaging 16.00 for the former and 26.12 for the latter. He found it hard to keep even this up in the 1999 season, averaging 12.00 with the bat and 32.72 with ball in hand. After that, things went limp for the poor lad. Although he appeared in the squad photo for 2000, hands demurely clasped behind his back this time, he didn't get a single outing in the first team, and when the 2001 family snapshot was taken, he'd vanished. Will 'e manage to reawaken his career? Who knows, but the answer is in his own hands.

'You Can't Get Better Games Than This'

Australia v South Africa, World Cup semi-final, Edgbaston, June 1999

This was one-day international number 1,483. Wisden called it 'not merely the match of the tournament; it must have been the best one-day international so far played.'

Four days before the semi-final, Australia met South Africa in a 'must-win' qualifying game and needed 271 in their fifty overs. Coming in with the Aussies at a tricky 48 for three, Steve Waugh on 56 gave a simple catch to Gibbs, who dropped it. Knowing that if Australia won this game they would immediately play South Africa again in the semi-final, he's alleged to have looked Gibbs in the eye and said, 'You've just dropped the World Cup, mate.' He finished on 120 not out and steered Australia home with two balls to spare.

Whether or not he made that remark, the Aussies excel at playing psychological games with their opponents. In the next four days they had few qualms in suggesting that South Africa choked when it came to big matches.

They didn't start the crucial semi-final like chokers. Winning the toss, they put Australia in and Shaun Pollock immediately whipped out Mark Waugh, caught behind off a lifter. Gilchrist and Ponting steadied things until a flurry of three more wickets brought Steve Waugh (56) and Michael Bevan (65) together to pull Australia back into the game. They put on 90 in 22 overs, before Pollock (five for 36) and Allan Donald (four for 32) returned with some devastating bowling to restrict the lower half of the order to little more than fifty runs. Australia were all out for a modest 213 in 49.2 overs. Had the mind games backfired?

The two teams had finished the qualifying rounds equal on points, but the Aussies had the fractionally better scoring rate of 0.19. This was only of consequence in the unlikely event of a tie. Facing a mere 213, this was the last thing on South African minds as they began their reply. They started well and had reached 48 comfortably enough before Shane Warne was brought on. Although in the game four days previously there were hints of his old form, Warnie had so far had a lacklustre tournament. That was all about to change. Reviving memories of his famous 'Gatting ball' of 1993, he warmed up with a huge leg break to bowl Gibbs, then trapped Kirsten and Cronje in quick succession. No runs, three wickets, and before they knew it South Africa were 61 for four.

They rallied well. Jacques Kallis (53) and Jonty Rhodes (43) scampered and improvised 84 off the next 19 overs, and Pollock broke Warne's stranglehold on one end with six and four off successive balls. With their downfall, though, the endgame was in sight. With 39 needed in 31 balls, South Africa's hopes rested on the heavyweight bat of Man of the Series, Lance Klusener. The tension tightened, and tightened again. Told afterwards the Aussies had looked pretty calm, Steve Waugh said, 'Jeez, is that what it looked like? Actually we were ******* ourselves out there, I can tell you.' When last man Allan Donald came in 16 were still needed, and seemingly Australia were home and dry. This was not how Klusener saw it. A ferocious six and a single took him to the striker's end for the last over. Nine wanted. Damien Fleming to bowl. Four through cover off the first ball, and another off the second. The scores were level with four balls remaining. Lord's was beckoning. Klusener blocked Fleming's third ball. The fourth was on a perfect length. Klusener pushed it towards Mark Waugh at mid-off, and charged up the pitch like a demented water buffalo. Donald started, stopped, dropped his bat, narrowly avoided death under Klusener's galloping hooves and finally set off for the other end. Too late. Waugh missed the bowler's stumps, but Fleming gathered the ball, rolled it down the pitch, overtaking Donald in the process, and Gilchrist whipped off the bails.

'It doesn't get more exciting than this,' said Cronje afterwards. 'It's unfortunate to be on the wrong side of it. At the moment it feels like a cruel game.' 'I'm almost sorry for South Africa,' said Waugh – with a commendably straight face.

Stick With Me, Baby, I'm the Feller You Came in With

Gavin Hamilton suffers a crisis of confidence, 1999–2002

Some unlucky golfers get the yips, particularly on the greens, and, with an inventiveness which Heath Robinson would applaud, devise outlandish putters (think of Sam Torrance and Bernhard Langer, for instance) to cope with the problem. Bowlers are sometimes similarly afflicted with a complete loss of confidence in their ability even to hit the pitch, let alone the stumps, but however tempting it might be to adopt a Roman catapult as an aid to overcoming the difficulty, umpires are less forgiving of novelties than golfing referees. Only rarely, though, does the condition become so extreme that a bowler simply refuses to carry on.

Born in Scotland but qualified for Yorkshire, 21-year-old Gavin Hamilton got his first couple of games for the county in 1996, took four wickets and made a fifty. 1n 1998 he consolidated his progress with a batting average of 33.6, and 56 wickets at 22.4, the second-highest wicket-taker for the county. This was a prelude to his *annus mirabilis* in 1999. As Wisden said of his achievements that year, 'he impressed with his utter determination', topping the Yorkshire batting averages at 47.25, the only player to exceed 40, and being second in the bowling averages with 43 wickets at 19.2. 'It seemed clear,' Wisden continued, 'that Hamilton would soon play international cricket, the only question being for whom.' New ICC rules meant that he 'could hope to be selected for England in the World Cup, or fall back on a certain place with his native Scotland otherwise'.

In the event, he contrived to play for both countries in 1999, his performances for Scotland leading to what Dr Johnson insisted was a Scot's best prospect, the road that led to England. Scotland didn't win a match in the qualifying rounds of the World Cup, but they showed plenty of fight and pushed both Australia and Pakistan harder than either can have expected for which Hamilton, 'on whom Scotland were heavily dependent', can take much of the credit. He scored exactly one-third of all Scotland's runs in the competition, including both his country's first half-centuries in international cricket, and finished in the competition's top twenty run-scorers, averaging 68.7. His bowling, meanwhile, achieved an admirably economical rate of only 3.4 an over. If his selection for England's 1999–2000 winter tour to South Africa was not necessarily a foregone conclusion, nor did it come as any great surprise.

The tour started comfortably enough for him. He played well in the warm-up games, and was duly selected for the first Test in Johannesburg – and that's where the wheels came miserably off his wagon. England made the worst start to a Test match first innings in history – two runs on the board and four wickets down – before Vaughan and Flintoff worked their way towards some sort of respectability. But poor Gavin Hamilton came away from England's massive defeat with a pair and nought for 63 in fifteen overs, and that, not surprisingly, was the effective end of his tour and, possibly, of his Test career.

Back on the county circuit, Hamilton's 2000 season was good enough, without hitting the heights of the previous year. His first championship century and 33 wickets at 24.8

suggested the horrors of his Test match experience had been laid to rest, but it was in 2001 that his confidence seemed to falter and go into decline. In his eight first-team games, he managed only 114 runs at an average of 12.7, and 26 wickets for 25.8.

It was in 2002 that the bowler's yips really set in. Against Surrey at the start of the new season he'd endured the harrowing experience of being unable to put the ball anywhere near the intended spot, and had withdrawn into the second team for seven weeks to try and iron things out. With sufficient confidence regained, or so it seemed, he was brought back into the first team for the game with Sussex at Headingley. Coming on first change, his 'public humiliation', as the *Telegraph* described it, continued. After a single over which conceded 17 runs, one no-ball and five wides, Hamilton removed himself to the deep field, in what must have been darkest despair, and bowled no more.

Other players have plumbed the depths and recovered their sparkle – Mark Butcher and Dominic Cork spring to mind – and everyone must hope, to misquote *Guys and Dolls*, that from now on luck will be a lady and never get out of Gavin's sight.

The Bombay Duck Gets
Five Gold Rings for Christmas

Australia v India,
December 1999–January 2000

As Agit Agarkar boarded the plane for India's visit to Australia in December 1999, world records did not weigh heavily on his mind. The year before he'd won his only cap so far, against Zimbabwe, and his ambition would be to secure a place in the Test XI with his ability to reverse swing the ball. In this respect he did well. He was India's leading wicket-taker in the three-match series, with eleven scalps including Steve Waugh on four occasions, and topped the bowling averages at 31.9. Nothing to start a forest fire down under, admittedly, but it was his batting that toppled world records.

Striding out at No 8 in the first innings of the first Test in Adelaide, he made 19, pretty much par for the course for a bowler with batting pretensions in domestic cricket. Coming in at 93 for six in the second innings he was caught off Damien Fleming and departed for a golden duck. Not much of a present with Christmas only ten days away, but never mind. In the second Test in Melbourne, the unusual began to become routine as Agit departed first ball in each innings, but he's a popular fellow in the Indian dressing room and the soubriquet of

170

Bombay Duck was probably the worst he had to endure. It was in the third Test that it started to get monotonous. Demoted to No 9, he trudged out to face Brett Lee and returned to the pavilion one ball later, having set an all-time Test record of four consecutive first-ball ducks. With power to add.

When he sidled to the crease in the second innings the score was 234 and Glenn McGrath was bowling. Triumphantly, he survived his first ball only to touch the second to Alan Gilchrist behind the stumps. He had now equalled another Test record – five consecutive ducks. Man, Courtney Walsh must be proud of him. By the time Agarkar reached England for the first Test at Lord's in July 2002, he had cranked his average up to 7.47. How did he celebrate? With a scintillating 109 not out as India crashed to defeat by 170 runs. The ugly duckling had become a swan.

Windies Uncorked at Lord's

England v West Indies, 2nd Test, Lord's, June 2000

The West Indies arrived in England in 2000 apparently on the mend. After nightmare series in South Africa (1998–9) and New Zealand (1999–2000), in which they had lost every Test played, they had soothed their nerves at home by beating Pakistan and Zimbabwe. Moreover, it had been 31 years since England had last won a series against the Windies, and in the history of meetings between the countries England had won only 28 Tests against the Windies' 51. Psychologically, England were conditioned to losing, and the challenge that summer was whether a 'new look' England could hold both their nerve and their opponents. It certainly didn't seem so in the first Test, in which England crashed to defeat by an innings. Their old tormentors, Courtney Walsh and Curtly Ambrose, beaming in anticipation, had them on the rack at once, shooting them out for 179 and 125.

Spectators arriving at Lord's for the second Test therefore wrapped round them their masochistic cloak of gallows humour and again prepared for the worst. At first, things went much as they expected. Just before tea, the West Indies were 161 for one, and the only wicket lost was to a run-out. Without warning, everything changed. Cork, returning to the England side, began banging the ball in short and dismissed both Campbell (82) and Hinds (59). Gough accounted for Lara and Adams, and the West Indies were 186 for five. They rallied to some extent and finished the day on 267 for nine, with Courtney Walsh proudly unconquered on a single.

As the crowds converged on Lord's next morning, they could not have guessed that they were to witness events that would enter the record books and help to earn the soubriquet 'epic' for this Test. To begin with everything was, as on the first day, routinely predictable. Courtney was dismissed first ball to close the Windies innings for 267, and within minutes of the start of play, the England openers were on their way in – and straight back out again. Even by the standards of the first Test, three wickets down for nine runs was not good. Although Hick (25), Stewart (28) and White (27) attempted to counterattack, England were bundled out for 134 in less than 49 overs. Walsh and Ambrose shared eight wickets between them, and it all seemed depressingly the same as ever. And then followed the most astonishing session of cricket an English crowd had seen for nearly twenty years. 'The balance of the match,' said Vic Marks, the former England spinner, 'lurched from one side to the other in the time it takes to munch a corporate lunch.'

Andy Caddick's bowling in the first innings had been unthreatening and uninspiring. Now, attempting to cut a near long hop, Campbell looped the ball off the edge towards third man where Gough took a brilliant catch. From that moment, Caddick was inspired. Bowling faster, much faster, than in the first innings he got steep lift from a length. Hinds fell to him at once. Six for two. Thus encouraged, Gough (two for 17) joined the party, and when he or Caddick took a breather Cork (three for 13) kept things boiling. Memories of their whitewashings in South Africa and New Zealand doubtless assailed the Windies batsmen and their innings simply cracked open.

Ten for three became 24 for five; then 39 for six became 39 for eight. Thanks to Walsh's inventive three not out, the West Indies scraped past their lowest ever Test score, but the unthinkable had happened, and in just two hours the West Indies were all out for 54. In thirteen devastating overs, Caddick had taken five for 16. Before close of play, there were seven deliveries in England's second knock so, for the first time in over 1,500 Tests, a part of all four innings had been played in a single day.

Next day, in an atmosphere of unbearable tension, England – just – got the 188 runs needed for victory. The Windies batting collapse changed the whole series. From then on, England batted with greater certainty, and the Windies did the opposite. Out for 61 in the fourth Test and 125 in the fifth, they surrendered the rubber 3–1.

Beware (Another) Baggy Greenwash!

South Africa v Australia, 1st Test, Johannesburg, February 2002

When the Proteas arrived down under in December 2001 for their three-match series with the Australians, the contest was billed as a titanic struggle for supremacy between the world's two best sides. In less than a month, it was all over. In three encounters, Australia had crushed South African aspirations by 246 runs, nine wickets and ten wickets respectively. The visitors had been outscored, outbowled and out-captained from first to last. The next step in what was to have been the battle of the heavyweights was slated for Johannesburg, with another three-match series commencing in South Africa in February 2002. Here, on their home ground, and with the satisfaction of having pushed the Aussies out of the triangular one-day competition and lifted the title, South Africa would be a different proposition. Wouldn't they?

Not if Steve Waugh and ten other steely-eyed Aussies had anything to do with it. To be sure, the Proteas didn't have too much luck. Opening bowler and skipper Shaun Pollock was unfit, and Allan Donald was injured in the course of the first day's play. Worse, they lost the toss and gave Australia first use of an excellent batting wicket. At the close of the first day, the visitors were 331 for five and for once the terrible twins, Langer and Hayden had 'failed', their opening partnership being a mere 46 on this occasion (though Matthew Hayden compensated by staying for 122). A score of 331 for five almost represented respectability from South Africa's viewpoint. A quick breakthrough in the morning and they would be back in the match...

Alas for self-delusion. When the breakthrough came there were only twenty minutes to go till tea and the scoreboard read 610. Damien Martyn (133) and Adam Gilchrist (204 not out) had put together a little matter of 317 – only 27 runs short of the world record sixth-wicket stand which Bradman and Fingleton had made 65 years earlier. Gilly surfed to his double-ton – at the time, the fastest in Test history – on a tsunami of 19 fours and 8 sixes in just 212 deliveries, eight fewer than Ian Botham had needed against India in 1982. South Africa were 'disembowelled' by Gilchrist, as the *Telegraph*'s correspondent noted. 'He wielded his bat like Luke Skywalker did his light-sabre in an innings of boundless audacity, superlative talent and hard-honed skill.' When Steve Waugh finally declared, at 652 for seven, Australia had made its highest-ever total against South Africa, a side which must have felt it had been shot from a cannon as it collectively staggered off the field.

In the circumstances, Herschelle Gibbs (34) and new cap Ashwell Prince (47 not out) did well to guide South Africa to 111 for the loss of only four wickets by the close of the second day, but when the Aussies have their opponents on the ropes, they don't let them escape. The third day saw a ruthlessly clinical knockout delivered as the Proteas were skittled for 159 and 133 to leave Australia winners by an innings and 360 runs, the second-biggest margin of victory in the whole history of Test cricket. Only England's win by an innings and 579 at the Oval in 1938 was bigger, and on that occasion two of the Australian batsmen, Bradman being one of them, had been too injured to go to the wicket.

The truth is that South Africa did not so much choke in the Johannesburg Test as become the victims of a clinical and ruthless strangler who knew his victim was frightened of him after the beatings handed out a few weeks earlier. In the two South African innings here, 54 per cent of the runs came from just two batsmen – Gibbs (28 per cent) and Prince (26 per cent) who together contributed 158 runs of their side's combined total of 292. New cap Prince, talented player though he is, had not been put through the Aussie mangle in the series down under, so his mind had yet to succumb to Steve Waugh's magnificent propaganda machine. As time goes by, it will be interesting to see how quickly he develops the mental strength to go with his skills.

Meantime, where is the side that can roll up its sleeves and face down the Aussie bullyboys? India managed it on their own turf not so long ago. Any other volunteers?

'Mark My Words, It'll Be a Lively First-Day Wicket'

Australia v England, 1st Test, Brisbane, November 2002

England were getting better and tougher. They were unlikely to win back the Ashes on Aussie soil, but they aimed to come away having improved on the single Test win they'd secured last time they were Down Under and, who knows, if they could rattle the Australian cage early, they might even take their formidable opponents by surprise and sneak a series victory. As Peter Perchard wrote in *Cricketer International*, 'If England can hit the ground running . . . then anything is possible.' One had only to think back to Mike Gatting's 1986 bunch of no-hopers, who'd trundled up to the Gabba in Brisbane on the back of eight defeats in their previous eleven tests against Australia, and a disastrous start to their tour, and had come away with a seven-wicket win which launched them on their triumphant way to Ashes success (see page 135). On that occasion, Border had made the horrible mistake of putting England in after winning the toss. Those with longer memories of the Gabba recalled Hutton's equally catastrophic decision to insert Australia way back in 1954 (see page 84), the punishment for which was to watch the hosts run up a meagre 601 for eight declared.

At least there was no danger of Nasser Hussain making that kind of mistake. In these enlightened days, when the ghosted newspaper column lays things bare almost before the lads in the dressing-room have twigged them, Nasser had assured us in the *Sunday Telegraph* that he was going to consult widely about how the Brisbane wicket would behave before walking out to toss the coin. It seems he failed to consult Typhoon Tyson, the main victim of Hutton's decision 48 years earlier. Tyson, who had emigrated to Queensland half a lifetime ago, wrote an article about the behaviour of the wicket for the *Daily Telegraph* two days before the first Test started. He left little room for doubt that if you win the toss at the Gabba you bat first.

Nasser also failed to consult Jeff Thomson, Australia's terrifying quickie from the 1970s, who played for Queensland and still lives there. Thommo pointed out on the radio that under normal circumstances the wicket retains moisture beneath a hard surface, and this water is brought to the surface by the heavy roller and causes problems on the first day of a game. However, as he went on to explain, current circumstances were very far from normal because Queensland had been suffering a prolonged drought, and it was common knowledge in Brisbane that the ground was bone dry as far down as you cared to dig. In other words, whatever you do, bat first if you get the chance to do so.

The great day of the first Test and a new Ashes campaign dawned with England – despite being without the injured Darren Gough and Freddie Flintoff – waiting 'to hit the ground running' and catch their formidable opponents on the back foot. The coin was tossed and Hussain called correctly. But he chose not to bat first, and shortly afterwards Justin Langer and Matthew Hayden emerged from the pavilion to begin Australia's first innings. Keen ears might have caught the laughter coming from their dressing-room. England helped them on their way with some appalling fielding and contrived to drop Hayden, the most in-form batsman in the world, three times as Australia powered to 364 for two at the close of the first day. England had one stroke of genuine ill fortune when their new fast-bowling hope, Simon Jones – who'd started well, with one for 32 from seven overs – suffered a terrible knee injury as his studs caught in the turf and put him out of the tour. The first day had been the worst of all nightmares. 'Australia might have been 300 for five or six at the close,' Hussain explained that night to a baffled press pack, who were left wondering how that would have caught the Aussies off guard.

England showed fight on the second day, as they whipped out the last eight Australian batsmen for 128 to limit the first innings total to 492, and then fought back with a second-wicket partnership of 121 between Marcus Trescothick and Mark Butcher. That was their high-water mark. They conceded a first-innings lead of 167, to which the Aussies added 296 for five declared to leave England facing Glenn McGrath, Jason Gillsepie and Shane Warne for four sessions on a pitch now cracking up. They didn't even make it as far as the fifth day, subsiding with a gentle wheeze to 79 all out in 28.2 overs. Vic Marks began his account of the debacle with the words: 'The match was over half an hour before it began. Hussain, by his own admission, made a terrible mistake at the toss.' He might as easily have said: 'The Ashes were lost half an hour before the series began.' To nobody's surprise, the Australians had the series wrapped up, with ease, within a month as England went three for nought down. If it is any consolation to him, which is doubtful, Hussain's name is now forever linked in the folklore of cricket with those of Hutton and Border.

Englishmen had only three crumbs of comfort – Michael Vaughan's magnificent three superb centuries in the series; the unquenchable cheerfulness of the faithful Barmy Army, who followed the team everywhere and brightened the lives of barmen across the breadth of Australia; and a consolation victory in the fifth Test. After annihilating South Africa and England in the space of twelve months, the inhabitants of Oz could be proud of one of the greatest cricket teams in the history of the game.

Postscript: An Encouraging Sign for the Future

The Rainbow Nation enjoys itself, Cape Town, 1 February 2002

You may or may not like pyjama cricket in all its technicolour-clad brilliance, but to be present at Newlands as the sun set behind Table Mountain, and see kids of all ages from five to fifty rush onto the field with their bats and balls during the dinner break of this day-night match, was a pleasure to be savoured.

The cricket was adequate, but not much of a contest. Western Province made 229 for four in their 45 overs, thanks to a splendid 117 not out by opener Graeme Smith on his twenty-first birthday. (At the time, I made a mental note that Smith might one day replace Gary Kirsten opening for South Africa, but didn't expect his first cap to be just five weeks later, against Australia, still less that within fourteen months he'd be made captain of his country.) No red faces among the Western Province batsmen, despite three of the four wickets being run-outs.

By contrast, North West's reply was a clanger from beginning to end. Opener Morne Strydom, taken aback by Alan Dawson's considerable pace, was caught behind off the first ball in a tangle of feet and bat. From there on, North West stumbled along at a run-rate of barely one an over, losing wickets all the way, until Western Province took pity, and by means of some friendly bowling at the death allowed them the partial respectability of 140 all out.

It was the dinner break that made the occasion memorable. On this venerable and beautiful Test match ground, the players had not left the field before there were impromptu games being played on every available square inch – as they used to be on English grounds before committeemen forgot that enjoyment and entertainment are what draw people through the turnstiles. Here, on this night, in a town with a long history of racial divide, small black boys and girls played with small white boys and girls; black and white teenagers hurled thunderbolts at each other and smote the ball lustily in all directions; white dads bowled to black kids and black dads bowled to white kids. People in the stands joined in the spirit of the thing, chasing after the balls as they whistled off the edge or were missed completely.

When the umpires returned, the games stopped and the ground cleared of its hundreds instantly. No bell was rung, no appeal had to be made. They simply went back to the Hill or into the stands, and the carnival continued there. Below me, a group of black and white girls in their twenties sang throughout North West's innings, pausing only to distract Graeme Smith whenever he happened to chase a ball in their direction. On the Hill, impromptu picnics and sing-alongs continued in any old colour medley. In the front row of the members' pavilion, four eight-year-olds, two white and two black, anxiously pooled their financial resources to invest in one cup of ice-cold chocolate milkshake, bought from one of the many circulating vendors crying their wares. Three rows behind me, one of the ice-cream sellers got into a lengthy and boisterous chat about the cricket with a couple he met. If there were any red faces that evening, they were red with exertion and pleasure.

If you had been lucky enough to enjoy the impartial *joie de vivre* of this night at Newlands – which never diminished the partisan support for the cricket in the middle – you could feel confident that cricket in the twenty-first century has a very real future. The rainbow crowd at the Rainbow Nation's most beautiful cricket ground has plenty to teach the rest of us. As one man, who told me he was classified a Cape Coloured in the bad old days, said to me with a twinkle, 'This couldn't have happened a few years ago. I'd have been arrested for talking to you. We'd all have been arrested.' This is neither to ignore nor downplay the many tough, very tough, miles South Africa still has to travel as it seeks to put the crude social engineering of apartheid behind it and become a viable nation of a different nature. But, on this one evening at Newlands, a cricket match was able to show how well we can reach out and communicate with each other – if only we have the confidence and freedom to be ourselves.